"I Have to Be Perfect"

(And Other Parsonage Heresies)

Timothy L. Sanford, M.A.

LLAMA PRESS
Colorado Springs, CO

ACKNOWLEDGMENTS

These are just some of the individuals who are partly to credit, or blame, for this book. They prodded, encouraged, edited, spell-checked, revived (me, that is!), pulled, pushed, suggested, critiqued, referred, advised, packaged, labeled, mailed and cheered. Without them I would have had more time in the mountains, but you wouldn't have this book in your hands.

Max Anders (minister)
Stephen Bransford (PK)
David (MK) Gatewood (MK and former missionary/minister)
Chonda Pierce (PK)
Ruth Van Reken (MK and missionary)
Grace Saenz (friend)
Becky Sanford (married to an MK, me!)
David (PK) and Karene Sanford (missionaries)
Heidi Sanford (daughter of an MK), now Heidi Peveto
Terryll Sanford (daughter of an MK), now Terryll Fleming

The many PK/MK clients/friends that I can't name because of confidentiality.

Thanks

TABLE OF CONTENTS

Foreword

I'm a comedienne. No, really, I am. I've always said if you grow up a southern preacher's daughter sitting on the second row; then almost nine times out of ten, you will become a preacher's wife – or a comedienne.

I'm a comedienne!

Growing up in the *stained glass jungle*, I have had some hilarious experiences – like the time when a visiting evangelist stayed in *my* room for a week and I went sleep-walking and wound up in the wrong bed. I was only four then and I really don't think it would have been that big of a deal, except that I was supposed to have been on my way to the bathroom.

Funny stuff? For me, growing up in the parsonage was filled with funny stuff. Yet, at the same time there are things that happened that weren't very funny at all, but then again we aren't suppose to talk about *those* times. Are we?

But Tim Sanford comes along and not only does he allow us to talk about some of the not-so-funny days, he *encourages* us to do so. Amazing! Because of this call to honesty, I have seen healing take place in the lives of adult preacher's kids – adults who, for years, have simply longed to be heard.

The first time I heard Tim Sanford was at an Adult Preacher's Kids Conference that I hosted in Nashville, Tennessee. For years he has worked as a professional counselor, but at the conference he was able to share with me and others a tremendous amount of knowledge, wisdom and insight slanted from the perspective of a preacher's kid – because he's one of us! Tim and I quickly became good friends. I taught him a couple of jokes and he taught me how to overcome some of the misconceptions that I have had about God and His church.

So if you are a preacher's kid looking for answers, or a pastor looking for some parenting tools for your parsonage family – or even a nosy layman wondering what makes us tick – then this book will open your heart and mind towards a wellness in Christ Jesus. And then, who knows, you might even become a comedienne! Or a preacher's wife!

Chonda Pierce
Comedienne/Recording Artist
Nashville, Tennessee

INTRODUCTION

Someone once asked me what being an MK (missionary's kid) was like. Bad timing, because they caught me in one of my more sarcastic moments. By the way, sarcasm is a PK (pastor's kid)/MK's second (or third) language! I told them that being an MK is a lot like being a white lab rat; everybody observes you, pokes at you, tests you, measures you, surveys you, but nobody wants to climb inside the cage and be your friend. No one is really able to see the world from your vantage point. No one is willing to touch the world that touches you or even listens to you describe it. Well, I'm already in the cage. Care to join me?

I'm not writing *about* PKs. I'm writing *to* PKs. To you. This is not a book to help others understand you better. It's a book to help you understand yourself better, or maybe for the first time.

> "New concept!" you're probably thinking. "You mean, pay attention to *my* needs and what makes me tick? Are you sure this is biblical?"

I assure you, it is.

I have been rubbing shoulders with PKs and MKs all of my life. I am related to approximately half of all the PKs or MKs in the world anyway! My dad is a PK, which makes his six brothers and one sister PKs. My grandmother began her fifteen-year missionary career as a widow, at the age of seventy. Four of my uncles were missionaries or pastors at one time or another, which makes all their children, my cousins, PKs/MKs. Several of my cousins have married PKs/MKs. (Interbreeding is common among the MK rat population!) Even some of my cousins have ended up in the ministry. Who knows, I may even be related to you!

I have been working as a licensed professional counselor with PKs and ministry families for many years. As I have listened to story after story, I've noticed several common themes and thinking patterns among PK/MKs. As I looked at my own life, some of those same thinking patterns raised their ugly heads in my mind too, much to my surprise. I thought my life was fine. I have good memories of my growing up years. I assumed then that my thinking patterns were normal. That I was mentally healthy. Not quite. It wasn't until a return trip to Ecuador a few years ago that I realized – allowed myself to recognize – there were negative and painful experiences as well. I had been playing the perfect MK role, verbalizing the good and repressing the bad. Along with the positive experiences, I still sustained damage from growing up in a ministry environment. Would I trade away my experience of being an MK? Never. Would I trade away some specific experiences I encountered? Yes, in a heartbeat.

My simplistic view has changed. I now see the damage left deep in my mind and heart. I remember reading books about what it's like living in a "glass house." That was good, but it didn't help me untangle my thinking. I found myself saying, "So what? Now what?" There's a high likelihood that you have experienced "occupational hazards" that come with your parents being in the ministry as well.

This book addresses the "What?" the "So what?" and the "Now what?" I want to help you uncover the *conclusions* you drew during those years in the rat lab, inside the glass house. I want to help you look specifically at the conclusions you may have drawn about yourself, the world and God.

One of the most profound things I remember from all my psychology courses is the truism, "Wherever you go, there you are." Believe me, it's doctrinally sound. I checked it out. You may be a long way away from a parsonage now, the experiences may be long forgotten, but the conclusions you formed in your mind are still with you today, whether you realize it or not. And most of us don't. Wherever you go, you take your mind with you (at least I *hope* you take your mind with you). You use your mind to interpret everyday events, filtering them through the conclusions you made many years ago.

Reading about the mind, beliefs, conclusions and thought patterns can get rather confusing in a hurry. Let me try to simplify the matter by using a word picture. I think in pictures anyway, so this works well for me. You won't find this in any psychology textbook, but it's true nonetheless. Picture your mind as a jukebox. A real jukebox - the old kind with vinyl 45s in them and a panel of buttons, each corresponding to a specific hit single. You can even watch the record drop down onto the pad, the arm swing over and the needle slip into the groove as it begins playing your selection. Some of us can remember when those were *not* called "antiques"! Anyway, that's what your mind is like. Each record has etched on it a sound recording of a simple, short phrase known as a belief. A belief is a statement of what you think is fact, a conclusion you hold onto about the circumstance you are facing. Most of your beliefs were recorded, catalogued and filed into your jukebox during the first seven to nine years of your life. Get the picture?

Religious beliefs are what you usually think of first when you hear the word belief. Actually, you have beliefs about every subject under the sun. You use those beliefs every day as you attempt to make sense of life. It's your world view so to speak, all on a bunch of 45s!

It plays out (no pun intended) like this:

>A new experience happens, or a set of similar experiences.

>>You attempt to understand this situation as best you can.

>>>You draw a conclusion from the experience about what is true, and thereby assume *will* be true in the future.

>>>>A recording of your conclusion is made into a belief statement and filed away in your jukebox. The new record is polished, catalogued and ready for future reference.

>>>>>Now, every time a similar situation arises, that record plays and you respond accordingly.

We all have one record that pretty much sounds the same. It's one that says "All my records, all my beliefs, are true. I can even validate them with real-life experiences!" I have also noticed that we are quite defensive of our set of records. If you disagree with me, my defenses come back shouting (at least in my head, if not out loud) "What do you think I am, stupid? I wouldn't believe a lie! I have intelligence too, I'll have you know. I *know* what is right and true, and I can back it up with experiences!"

If you are willing to get past your knee-jerk defensiveness, you may find some of your records a bit warped. The conclusions you drew as a child may not have been based on complete information. The beliefs you live and die by may not be totally accurate. They may have *seemed* accurate at the time, and may have been partly or mostly true, *then*. But not now. Not when compared to the larger realm of reality. But the records remain in the slots of your jukebox, warped and inaccurate, waiting to be activated by the touch of a button, even today. When one of your not-so-accurate records gets triggered and plays, it sounds funny to everyone else but you. To you, it sounds true, even today. Most of us never stop long enough to question whether or not our beliefs are accurate. We just believe they are. I'm sure my jukebox theory is what stimulated the phrase, "Man, you're really warped in the head!" I can't prove it, but I'll take credit for it anyway. Where was I? Oh yeah.

This book is a collection of what some of those warped records sound like. Records that I have heard played over and over again by PKs across the country. I call them the holy heresies of the parsonage, because that's exactly what they are. You may have detected a bit of sarcasm here, but I also know the truth in that old Chinese saying, "Many a truth is said in jest." The good news is that warped records *can* be straightened out or replaced. The bad news is, it takes some honest introspection to find them. It is my hope that you will look seriously at the records in your jukebox to see if any of them are warped. I hope you will take time to question the conclusions you drew subconsciously long ago. Some of them may need to be updated and changed. I hope you will check to see if you have any holy heresies floating around your doctrinally pure, innocent PK mind. Besides, your jukebox probably is in need of a good cleaning anyway! Clean jukeboxes sound better. Clean minds think better. Sounds real therapeutic, doesn't it?

Whenever someone begins to talk about pastors or ministry leaders of any kind, they must run through a series of disclaimers first. After all, talking negatively about a pastor is the same as disparaging God himself, isn't it? You know what I mean, all the "What I'm *not* saying" kinds of things. We can't have anybody's toes stepped on, now can we?

So, in order to be religio-politically correct and doctrinally pure, here are the necessary disclaimers:

(1) I am *not* here to blast pastors, church leaders or denomination officials. I *am* here to try to help you look deeply and truthfully at your own life and experiences. (Repeat first stanza.)

(2) I am *not* giving you an excuse to blame someone else for your own choices and actions.

(3) I am *not* here to sugarcoat things or gloss over the real issues. Sometimes the truth does in fact hurt. This is not Sunday school or choir practice. PKs are used to pretending; we are used to covering up and looking "good", so much so that we often begin to believe it ourselves. Well, *not* here.

(4) I am *not* assuming that every pastor's family is nutty and screwed up. I am *not* assuming all PKs are basket cases or "warped in the head." I am *not* assuming that all was well on the parsonage porch, either.

There, that about covers it - at least for the Introduction.

WARNING LABEL to you (church leaders, parents, professionals or spouses) who want to better understand PKs: It's difficult to truly understand the world of the PK unless you are one. It's different being in the ministry as an adult than being a child with your parents in the ministry. As a minister you chose the ministry; your kids had no choice. As pastor you have adult coping skills to deal with the occupational hazards of the ministry; your kids only have a child's level of abilities and skills.

If you work with PKs in a lay or professional setting, listen first, draw them out, try to learn rather than teach, then listen some more. Be aware of your *own* tendencies to covertly stereotype. You don't know our world, so please don't pretend to.
If you're married to one, heaven help you!

WARNING LABEL NUMBER TWO to you who want to understand MKs better: MKs are even more complicated to understand and work with. Unless you have been raised as a TCK (Third Culture Kid) you will not understand completely. This is not a smug statement, just a true one. Again, being the missionary is not the same as being the MK.

To you mental health professionals: Intercultural counseling is a *specialty*. Don't try to fit the TCK into your existing theoretical framework. It won't work. What you think may be dysfunctional may be a matter of your own cultural perception. Don't practice outside the scope of your expertise.

HOUSEKEEPING NOTE: Rather than constantly using PK/MK throughout the book, I've decided just to use PK. The content is fitting for both groups equally. Since the MK has the additional dynamic of culture to deal with, culture most often takes center stage. It's time to put the cultural issues on the back burner for a while and look at other issues that also impact MKs.

I've covered all the necessary formalities, so if you're still with me, let's go on. The rats are getting restless!

PART I:

WHAT'S THE PROBLEM...
ANYWAY?

BREAKING THE SILENCE

WARNING: If you're like me and tend to skip the Introduction part of a book, don't! Go back and read it. It sets the stage for understanding all that is to follow. Really.

A Look Inside
CHAPTER 1

One of the hardest words for many PKs to say is the small, simple word …

"*AND*"

How many times would it have been helpful, even accurate, for you to say, "*and*"?

- There were good times … *and* … there were hard times.
- Dad was a good dad … *and* … he made some mistakes too.
- I'm proud of our mission agency … *and* … they have made some bad choices along the way.

"*And*". A powerful and often honest word. Wasn't there the:

- Good and the bad?
- Fun mixed with the sad?
- Things done right as well as things done wrong?
- The godly and the selfish?

Several years ago I was speaking at a church-sponsored workshop here in Colorado Springs. At one of the breaks, I was approached by a woman in her thirties. I don't remember her name, so I will refer to her as Janie. Her ears had perked up when I shared some of my MK experiences in South America. A second generation MK from somewhere in the Far East (I can't remember this part either) who is now married to a pastor, Janie seemed ready to burst. She was emotionally starving for a chance to say the simple word *"and"* to someone without being labeled or rebuked. She did not hate the mission agency, nor her parents or the fact that she was an MK. She was very loyal to all three. But she merely wanted the freedom to say that there were painful times too, that the mission was not always perfect in its decision-making. But she couldn't. The mission would not tolerate such a thing, unofficially, of course. (We will take a deeper look at this phenomenon in chapter ten.) As we talked, Janie shared experience after experience, glad to have a safe place to tell the truth. She didn't need therapy. She needed the freedom to verbalize the *"and"*.

"And" requires you to be honest, at least with yourself. Many of the PKs I've talked with have been trained to "bear with the failings of the weak" and to "think (*only*) about such things" that are "lovely ... admirable" or "praiseworthy." These statements may sound spiritual, but they're incomplete in and of themselves. I'm sure the Pharisees thought they were spiritual and righteous too as they flaunted one part of the law and neglected other parts. If you want to believe these half-truths, be my guest. I'm sure God will think it perfectly saintly that you overlook the two drops of arsenic in the champagne in order to focus on the nice bubbles.

Most PKs I know have never ended up in the psychiatric unit of a hospital or behind prison bars, although I have talked with some in both of these places. But just because you may not have spent time in either of these institutions doesn't mean you automatically have a clean bill of health. PKs are good at adapting. We have to be. You may have learned to adapt so well that everyone sees you as normal because you act normal. You may even come to believe the half-truths completely yourself. Behind the adapting though, you may be hiding a world of hurt, pain, confusion, anxiety and warped thinking. Adapting has helped you survive, but it's not synonymous with good mental or emotional health.

Honesty is hardest off-stage. It's a balancing act, never an either/ or. Some of the parsonage rules sound very much like the rules in the house of a "drunken heathen." "Don't think," really. "Don't feel," pretend. "Don't talk," family secrets, you know. Before you think that was not your house, stop and let it soak in. It may be more true than what you want to admit.

"And" is an all-important word that can drastically change the tenor of a sentence. The *"and"* in the sentence for one teenage girl who sat in my office with a big black shiner under her right eye went something like this:

> "My dad (youth pastor) was in church last Sunday saying how he loves kids
>
> *… and …*
>
> the night before he beat me up and gave me this black eye."

I saw her black eye! Her mother confirmed the story. Sometimes *"and"* can sober up a conversation very quickly. But, so often, the *"and"* goes unspoken. *"And"* allows you to break the code of silence, to finally tell the secrets that really *need* to be told. I don't care how much this girl's dad says he loves kids, that is *not* how you treat a kid, ever, *ever!* I have a hard time believing the words when the fists are saying something different. In this case, pastor-dad's fists spoke a whole lot louder than even his finest Sunday morning sermon.

> **DEFINITIONS:** Family secrets. *Secrets* are when those who need to know, don't. *Confidentiality* is when those who need to know do. Those who don't, don't. Secrets need to be broken. Honest. Find someone who's trustworthy. Take the risk slowly, but take it. That someone may be a parent, a sibling, a spouse, a trusted friend. It may need to be a professional. Whatever it takes, secrets need to be shared. Honest.

Carefully think over what I'm saying. You may end up like the PK who called and said he had a letter ready to mail me that began, "Thanks for ruining my life!" He went on to say that he, too, thought everything was fine and wonderful in his PK experience. He was not abused or orphaned and never ended up in a gang. All was well (not to mention the history of depression and self doubt), until he began to look below the surface. He had become a professional adapter, a professional pretender. As he began to be honest with himself, for the first time in his life, he realized many of the holy heresies had crept into his thinking and had wreaked havoc in his life. He was crushed at first. He finished the conversation by telling me he was glad for the jolt and the chance to look deeper. After seeing things clearly, he was able to begin working on the issues that had kept him a prisoner all these years. He had begun his quest for freedom.

As you read on, you may wonder if I have met *any* PKs that are okay. Yes I have, all three of them! No, really, many PKs I've met are healthy and okay. I am purposely focusing your attention on the statements whispered after the "*and*" because these are the words that get overlooked or silenced. These words hold the pain, the hurt and the disappointment you may be living with all these years. It's these words, when stuffed or silenced, that bring on isolationism, bitterness, depression and/or anger.

Just because not everything was good does *not* mean everything, therefore, was bad. Addressing the difficult things, the painful things, the wrong things or the disappointing things you may have experienced does *not* nullify the positive, the fun, the enjoyable and the nurturing experiences. Here again, we fight the tendency to see the PK experience, and this book, with an either/or mind set. We have to fight to keep the "*and*" in the sentence, even when talking among ourselves.

Whether your PK experience was 95 percent healthy and 5 percent hassle, or if it was 80 percent hell and 20 percent heaven, be willing to take a hard, honest look at yourself and your thinking. The "*and*" is true; there was both in all our families and experiences. I have seen the hurt, anger and lost-ness in enough eyes over the years. I don't want you to be another silent casualty. Go through this book slowly and thoughtfully. Take what fits and throw away what doesn't. It may be a good idea to journal while you read. Write down what coincides with your life, what fits or what memories it summons. Document your thoughts, your feelings and any recollections that come to mind. Include your talks with God on the subject too (assuming the two of you are still on speaking terms). Strive to be genuine and honest. See how closely the journal pages match what is going on between your ears. Check out the Appendix, entitled, "Ideas for Keeping a Journal."

In addition, I've enclosed several worksheets throughout the book that may be helpful. Use the ones you like and skip the ones that don't scratch where you itch right now. Don't tear them out, because they just might be useful later on. Maybe …

Sometimes the truth hurts. If it needs to, let it.

The Forces That Impact You
CHAPTER 2

When most people think of belief systems or hear me talk about holy heresies, they automatically assume there will be an all-out attack on the family. After all, didn't you learn everything, good and bad, from your home environment? Close, but no cigar. Parents get a lot of blame, due and undue, and there is many a pew-sitter just waiting for some juicy morsel of gossip to pass along about the pastor's family. The truth is however, that there are more voices in your jukebox than just those of your mother or father. You have influences upon you from your family, the Christian community and your culture. All three have their voices imbedded deeply in your jukebox.

Family Forces

The family *does* play a *big* part in shaping your view of things. Many of the statements on the records of your mind were recorded in the home. So it's the logical place to begin.

The family is the "micro-culture," the smallest grouping of the three. The family is the "we" of individual relationships. The family is where the influences that come through the community and culture are fine-tuned and finalized. It's the force closest to you, but not the only powerful one.

What "*and*" statements are accurate about your family? What did mom and dad teach by way of their actions and the things they did not say? Resist the tendency to assume other PKs had the same kind of parents and family life you had. I have seen pastor/dads at every point along the continuum, from saints to psychopaths. I have heard of moms who are genuinely heavenly and others who are histrionic. It is estimated that 80 percent of today's ministers come from dysfunctional families.[1] Holy cow! Sounds like an udder disaster to me! Sometimes truth *is* stranger than fiction, even in the hallowed halls of the sanctuary.

What unspoken expectations did the family have? What was the image your family was expected to uphold? Were you allowed to speak up, really? Were you permitted to have and express *all* emotions? Were you listened to? Did you have a dad or a pastor in your home? You are going for honesty here, not "roast dad" (another one of those disclaimers). But for some of you, these questions have never been formulated in your mind. You never stopped to give them serious thought.

Out in public, these negative behaviors are nowhere to be found. But in the privacy of the parsonage, where only you could see, hear and feel, were they present? Some may have been present, others not. Some may have been present most of the time, some only occasionally. Poison is bad no matter the quantity or the frequency. Unsafe people are unsafe, even if it's only sometimes.

Your family, like every other family, had its good and its bad, maybe even safe times and unsafe times. The important thing is for you to see it as it really was. Once you see clearly, then you can take whatever action may be necessary. Ignorance is not bliss any more than signing a contract without reading it constitutes trust.

Church Community

The community is the "subculture" to which your family belongs. It further defines you and your family. Community is the social group, the larger collective. Ah yes, the infamous *they*.

> **RABBIT TRAIL:** Who are *they* that we spend so much of our time and energy worrying about, trying to please or trying to hide from? Ever notice how *they* have no specific names or faces? *They* never say anything right to your face. *They* are the nebulous group of who-knows-whos that watch us, evaluate us, judge us and somehow ended up with the power to validate or invalidate us. *They* have the power to accept or reject us.
>
> *They* make up the invisible group that makes up the "us" – the group that is greater than the sum of its membership. That's why there are no exact faces or voices. It's the collection of unwritten rules, expectations, threats and rewards used to make you conform to fit the corporate image.

The Christian community, in the form of the local church, the denomination, the para-church organization or the mission compound, is the most underestimated force of all on your belief system. From the denomination's top leaders to the gossips in the Fellowship Hall (Isn't that name a kick? "Fellowship," where more talking-about-people-behind-their-backs takes place than any other place on the church grounds!), the community has a profound impact on its members, especially you. The power of a group is almost unbreakable. That's true, from the Jim Jones cult tragedy to an Olympic sports team. Why do we think the group called the church is any different? I learned at a very young age that people would listen to my dad preach, and then give money for our support in direct proportion to how I behaved in the pew.

My dad never taught me that. My mom never suggested that. The pew-sitters, the holy church of God taught me that. Maybe you never thought about it this way, but PKs have 100 fathers and 150 mothers. You bet we do! No wonder we turned out so perfect!

> **SIDE NOTE** to you parents of PKs: You shared (or are sharing) your parenting influence with the church congregation. Whether it's right or fair or not, it's true. The local flock has become the PKs' unofficial extended family. And it's a silent, yet strong influence, both on thinking and behavior. It's one of the occupational hazards you put on your kids. Be aware, you share your parenting role with whoever enters the doors of your auditorium. Like it or not, you have to live with it, and so do your children.

> **CHALLENGE** to you parishioners: What you think, what you say, the non-verbal gestures you make about the pastor's kids get noticed. Do you notice the PK's hemline but not those of the other girls? Do you notice how fast the minister's son drives out of the parking lot, but overlook your own son's style of driving? Think about it before you answer.

Chonda Pierce, a comedienne, PK and friend of mine, tells the story of when she was about five years old. She was getting a drink from the water fountain one Sunday between Sunday school and church service. There were two elderly women in line behind her. One reached out and patted Chonda on the head and said to the other, "This is one of our preacher's daughters. She's not very p-r-e-t-t-y." Chonda, being the spunky person she is, even at age five, turned around and calmly replied, "No, but I'm real s-m-a-r-t!" PKs aren't dumb, deaf or blind. By the way, neither is God. You are accountable for the impact, verbal or otherwise, that you have on the PKs of your church.

Least I sound like a disgruntled PK looking to vindicate myself and further my own agenda, take a look at what Stephen Arterburn and Jack Felton, in their book *Toxic Faith*, describe as an unsafe church setting. Here are their "10 Rules of a Toxic Faith System":

1. Control – The leader must be in control at all times.
2. Blame – When problems arise, find a guilty party to blame immediately.
3. Perfectionism – Don't make mistakes
4. Delusion – Never point out the reality of a situation.
5. Perpetual Cheerfulness – Never express your feelings unless they are positive.
6. Blind Loyalty – Don't ask questions, especially if they are tough ones
7. Conformity – Don't do anything outside your role.
8. Mistrust – Don't trust anyone.
9. Avarice – Nothing is more important than giving money to the organization.
10. Spotless Image – At all costs, keep up the image of the organization or the family.[2]

Do any of these rules fit the church or churches you grew up in? Was there absolute leader control, even though the jargon sounded something like "servant leadership?" Was there blind loyalty? Was there a need to keep up the "image"? Was it expected of you? Was there a written or unwritten rule to conform ... or else?

Some years ago I was in Mexico as part of a mountain climbing group. One of our goals was the 18,851-foot summit of El Pico de Orizaba. The day before we arrived, there had been an accident involving three climbers. Several of us attempted a rescue. When we arrived at the site where the three climbers were, one was already dead. He had sustained massive internal head injuries during the tumble down the 2,000-foot icy slope. A second climber died right in front of me within five minutes after our arrival. The remaining climber was successfully stabilized and transported off the glacier where he was evacuated by helicopter the following day. As we were all trying to make sense of this tragedy, deal with our own emotions, and get some sleep, each of us individually decided not to attempt the climb the next day. Each of us vowed to stay at the refuge while the others went for the summit. When the alarm went off at 3:00 in the morning, the group began to rise; not a single climber said "no." We all dressed. We all packed our gear. We all headed out the door. The power of the group had sucked us in and we all went off into the brisk pre-dawn air in search of the summit, disregarding the individual choices we had already made.

Don't think for a moment that the Christian community is any less powerful. How safe was the community you grew up in? How much toxic faith was slopping around the Sunday school classrooms or board meetings?

Culture

If the Christian community is the most underestimated force, culture is the most overlooked force of the three. This largest impacting force, which I call the "macro-cultural," brings structure and order to your community, your family and yourself as an individual. It influences how you define your physical, psychological, religious and social needs. It defines how you view beauty and decide what you like and dislike. It also defines language – the way you communicate with the rest of the world, from your family members to your fellow countrymen.

What kind of impact has culture had on you? It may surprise you. What about *indirect* impact? The culture impacts the Christian community, which impacts you. The society has a large impact on the family, which in turn impacts you, too. How much do you think like an American (if you *are* an American, that is)? How much does your family and church think American (ditto)? If you ever get a chance to have an in-depth talk with people from a different culture, do it. It may help open your eyes to the impact your culture has had on you. Even if you have to pay for the lunch, ask them how they view American culture and its impact on you.

I realize there is more and more information coming out to help MKs sort out our unique identities as Third Culture Kids. I'm encouraged to hear more and more mission agencies addressing our needs. It's about time. It's also good to know that just because there are these funny brown spots on my white rat fur, I'm not totally alien!

You need to be aware of the forces that have impacted your thinking, which forged the records in the jukebox of your mind. Any and all of these forces can pass along holy heresies.

Notes

1. H.B. London, Jr. and Neil B. Wiseman, *Pastors at Risk*, (Wheaton, IL: Victor Books, 1993), 45.

2. Stephen Arterburn and Jack Felton, *Toxic Faith*, (Nashville, TN: Oliver-Nelson, 1991), 263.

"I Have to Be Perfect"
CHAPTER 3

Like a good evangelist, I'll go straight for the heart. "I have to be perfect" is a heresy so broad and so deep it takes many forms and disguises. I have heard too many PKs repeat these exact words. Others, who deny it with their words, prove it by their behavior patterns and thinking even if they don't see themselves as being perfectionists. Like any heresy that is worth its ink on onion skin paper, "I have to be perfect" has many variations. All of which can hurt deeply.

"Of course I have to be perfect. Let me count the reasons why!"
- Everybody expects me to be the shining example of whatever dad preaches.
- If I'm not, it's because I'm being irresponsible.
- Because I don't want to let my parents down.
- Because then I'll be letting God down.
- Things just go easier for everybody if I am perfect.
- I don't want to turn anybody off to the salvation message.
- Image is everything, that's what mom always says.
- The congregation will like dad better if I am.

Is there anything you want to add to this list?

An interesting twist to this heresy is that *you* are the only one bound by it. Others don't have to be perfect. Just you. Others are allowed to be human and make mistakes, but you aren't. "Others may, you cannot." Ever heard this? More on this in chapter six.

Perfectionism creates a goal that is both unattainable and non-existent. We couch it in nice Christian terms, as if that will make it more attainable somehow, if we are just disciplined enough, and trust in God enough, and if … and just … To keep us pursuing this absurd goal of perfectionism, we internalize a complex system of *should* statements that act like a pseudo-Holy Spirit – a tyrant dictator whose sole task is to keep us in line, a perfect line, that is.

- "I *shouldn't* have said that."
- "I *should* be more patient."
- "I *shouldn't* be so tired."
- "I *should* …"

Hear it? Whether you actually say the exact word or not, is it present in your thinking? By the way, who said that's the way it *should* be?

Perfectionism creates an unattainable goal, which then causes you to create the long list of *should* statements. But *should* is a good thing to say, right? It keeps you from doing something wrong and stupid, right? It keeps you responsible, right? Sure it does. Just like tying your two-year-old to the bedpost so she won't burn her pretty little hands on the kitchen stove. It works, but that is hardly the way to keep her safe.

With *should* thinking, you only have two options: The *should* way or the wrong way. Not only on the major issues of Scripture where there is genuine right and wrong, but it gets generalized into every part of life. This either/or mind-set is the catalyst for anxiety. Oh, I forgot, as believers we don't have "anxiety," we just call it concern. Don't buy it. It is the same horse, just a different color.

Now, as an adult, you find yourself making decisions based on what you're afraid of.

- Afraid of failing.
- Afraid of what others will think.
- Afraid of rejection.
- Afraid of not knowing something.
- Afraid of being irresponsible.
- Afraid of letting God down.
- Afraid … Afraid …

Afraid, all because somewhere deep inside you feel obligated to be perfect. Sound familiar? Would your spouse say it sounds familiar? Would your close friends say this chapter fits you? Remember, perfectionism comes from many directions and with many faces. Your closet may be a mess, but perfectionistic thinking may still be in your mind.

Not only does the need to be perfect generate a whirlwind of anxiety, it also destroys your self-confidence.

When everything is either *should* or fail,

you end up failing often,

which makes *you* a failure, or so you reason,

which makes you a stupid jerk,

which erodes your self-confidence.

27

At this point, you have two options, again. Option one is to die trying … trying … trying to be perfect. You may even distort reality so you at least feel successful. The other option is to quit and walk away. "If I don't try," you say to yourself, "I can't fail." You create an alibi that allows you to save face. Better to not try and fail, than to try your hardest and still come up short, right? All of this from the heresy that says, "I have to be perfect."

Excellence is fine. Passion for the work of God is great. Perfectionism, though, kills.

As a lab rat, I'm motivated by rewards. I also intensely avoid pain. I can live with either or both of these. But if you electrocute me for every little thing I do that isn't quite perfect, I'll end up neurotic, violent or catatonic! The same is true for humans.

The anxiety, mixed with damaged self-confidence, makes you a prime candidate for major depression. Back in 1996, I was giving a workshop entitled, "Inside the Mind of the PK" at the First Annual Adult Preacher's Kid Conference in Nashville. One of the PKs sitting in the front row asked me about PKs and depression. I asked for a show of hands of anyone who had been diagnosed with depression, placed on anti-depressant medications, or hospitalized for depression. Out of the 100 adults present, nearly 80 raised their hands. The evidence hit me like a train. Then a woman in the back of the room said it all; "Yeah, but we're not allowed to be!" Ouch! But how true.

Any of this sound familiar?

> **STUDY NOTE:** These heresies tend to be interrelated. As you read through these chapters, cross-reference back and forth as you feel the connections. Where there is one heresy, there may be more.

"I Should Already Know"
CHAPTER 4

The best place to begin talking about this particularly sneaky heresy is with me. As far back as I can remember, I have always believed that "I should already know" everything necessary to handle the situation in front of me. I should know the answer to the Sunday school teacher's question. I should already know how to handle a certain conflict. Disregard the minor fact that I have never come across any situation like this before, I still should at least know. I could write a book on all the things I *think* I should already know!

This heresy is not confined to religious matters. Years ago, when I was a wilderness guide, I had a chance to take a kayak run down the Arkansas River. As we worked on the technique of keeping this funny little boat right side up in the practice pond, I worked hard to master it. The "I should already know" began creeping in. After all, I was athletic. I was a wilderness guide. I had been down the river many times (in a raft, with a river guide). I thought, "I *should know* how to maneuver this contraption." As we put in the river for the "real thing," my goal was to do the entire piece of river without flipping over. After all (again), I *should know* how to handle this thing. Keep in mind that I had never been in a kayak before in my life … ever. But the "I should already know" doesn't take those small realities into account. It wasn't more than thirty seconds, yes *seconds*, after putting in that I flipped my kayak! The frustration I felt was not because of the awkwardness of trying to get out of a kayak that had flipped in only three feet of water, it was because I had failed at *already knowing* how to kayak. The "I should already know" heresy can attack any place, any time and in regard to any subject. By the way, after that spill, I made the rest of the run without flipping. The initial "failure" broke the "I should already know" self-expectation and freed me up to enjoy the experience.

A variation of this heresy is the conclusion that says, "I should be farther along in my spiritual journey than I am right now." Whatever it is, I should already know. Wherever I am on my spiritual journey, I should be farther.

This is a thinking pattern few non-PKs can really understand. They can't understand why we would even think this way. I'm not sure I understand either, but I *should* understand. I can't connect it with any event or circumstance that I can remember. What I think happened is that this heresy mutated through a pattern of interactions that went something like this:

> People knew I was an MK and assumed that I already knew more than the rest of the children.

> > I picked up on their assumptions and concluded that maybe I really *was* supposed to already know. So, instead of looking stupid, I pretended to know.

> > > They saw me pretending, concluded that I really *did* know, and continued to assume.

> > > > I continued to pretend …

When you are in this cycle, it creates four problems. First, you get good at pretending and hiding the truth. See how easily this can get intermingled with the heresy, "I have to be perfect"? You then get proficient at what I call duck-and-cover. This lack of genuineness hurts your own emotional and spiritual growth. You may even get good enough at pretending that you begin believing it yourself.

Second, you tend to not ask for assistance. After all, why ask for help on something you *should already know* how to handle? Why should you show everyone that you do *not* know what you should *already* know? You go through life on your own, by your own wits, silently watching others, but not asking for help.

Third, the other side of not asking for assistance is that others tend not to *offer* assistance either. Have you ever been asked if you want to be mentored by someone in the church? Have you ever been asked if you could use a friend and encouragement partner? If you are partially isolated by your lack of initiation, the isolation circle is completed by others not reaching out to you and offering help. You feel isolated, alone, and *different* (you will see this issue again in chapter six).

The fourth reason is probably the most damaging. With the "I should already know" comes the reality that I *do not* already know a lot of things. It's a shoe-in for self-contempt to rear its ugly head and swallow you whole. "I should already know ... but I don't, stupid." You start thinking you're a failure, and it's easy to embark on a mental-flogging program to get you back on track and acting the way you *should,* whatever that may be, even though you have no idea how. And you can get very skilled at beating up on yourself with words. You call yourself names. You recite belittling phrases to yourself in the catacombs of your mind. You conclude you're a jerk or a loser.

I have talked to some PKs who took self-contempt one step

further and physically beat up on themselves for feeling so stupid or incompetent, all because they think they *should already know*. You may be guessing I'm talking about gory slit wrists or another unhealthy way to cope with the not knowing what I think that "I should already know". PKs after all, have to be, or at least look, perfect. It would be totally unacceptable to go to church with scarred wrists, in full view of everyone! Think of what the Jones' would say! The offering would be less! The world would come to an end! So would dad's marvelous ministry!

"Oh, mercy! Did you see that, Ethel?"

The physical damage I'm talking about is most always hidden. Being good at covering up comes with good pretending. It may involve cutting, but in places where clothing always covers. It may take the form of physically working out to the point where it will actually do damage to the body. Another big way to physically hurt the body is through eating, or not eating. It's a great way to hurt yourself, without being found out. More on this in chapter ten.

> **REMINDER:** This heresy, like the others, has at least some truth to it. We are to be responsible, wise and competent, yes. We are to learn from our mistakes and endeavor to not repeat them, yes. But that is different from the heresy that says, "I should *already* know." It is simply and profoundly not true.

But it feels true.

But it's not.

But it seems true.

But it's *not* true!

You only know what you know today, and that is acceptable for today. You will learn more; you will be farther along tomorrow than you are today. But for today, it's okay. And it's enough, for today.

"I'm Here for Others"
CHAPTER 5

READING TIP: This heresy is usually accompanied by the heresy that says, "Other people's needs are more important than my own" that will be discussed in chapter nine. They are bedfellows (I like that word) and are a very dangerous one-two combination. You may want to flip back and forth between the two chapters as you read. It's allowed, you know.

The theme hymn for this heresy is "Channels Only." The banner verse is "Bear ye one another's burdens" (KJV). Growing up around the ministering mind-set can easily program you to think a cascade of thoughts such as:

I'm here to be a spiritual garden hose. You know, pass the "living water" from God on to others.

But the hose isn't important, and neither am I, just other people.

I only exist to serve others.

You may think it's your job, yes, even your calling or obligation, to make other people happy and comfortable. After all, they are the ones being ministered to, right? It's selfish of you to hinder "God's work" with your own needs, right?

Lie … lie … lie! …

But a lie never sounded so … so spiritual!

You remember the sermons. You should "look not … on your own interests, but … to the interests of others." Never mind the words "only" and "also" that get left out while quoting Philippians 2:4. We are to "carry each other's burdens." Half true. But half-truths are as damaging as whole lies. If you hold this line of thinking, consciously or not, you are throwing spiritual gutter balls on heaven's bowling alley, assuming they play tenpins in heaven. You may have adopted this position in order to not look selfish or ego-centered, the other bowling alley gutter. You have overcompensated to the extreme, but you are *still* putting the ball in the gutter. Being selfish or arrogant is wrong. Discounting the value God has for you is equally wrong. If the game is the same in heaven as it is downtown, either gutter nets you the same number of points. Zero.

Your legitimate needs go unmet, so you either end up depressed (here's the "D" word again!) or you try to salvage some feel-good feelings by holding onto a sense of self-righteousness. Silently you chalk up how many times you have sacrificed for the sake of the Gospel, and somehow try to fill the gaping holes in your soul that way. Either way, though, you lose. You lose having your own needs met. You lose a healthy sense of self. You lose your grip on the truth. This will come up again in chapter ten.

My dad recounts the time when his grade school Bible club leader asked him to stop memorizing any more verses until some of the other kids could catch up with him. The other club kids were discouraged since he, the preacher's son, was so far ahead of them in the memory competition. He *should* be expected to put the needs of others ahead of his own. Respect for leadership and deference to others were cardinal values in my grandparents' home. The minister, and his family, were there for others. The club leader's request was honored. With only a few weeks left before the competition was to end, the teacher promised she would let my dad know when someone got close to the number of verses he had memorized so he could resume his memory work. But she forgot. Her own son, my dad's very close friend, ended up winning the coveted prize!

It was a very disappointing ending to the story for the boy who so eagerly looked forward to a prize he could have easily captured, but lost. Dad admitted to having forgotten about the incident (after some time passed first). The story picked up twenty-five years later when my dad met up with the Bible club leader again. She apologized profusely for taking advantage of his willingness to respond positively to her request and put "others over himself." Forgiveness was extended, tears shed, and the pain in this lay leader's heart was relieved by a hug.

I saw the impact of this in the eyes of a teenage PK with whom I was working several years ago. She sat in my office with a demeanor of someone simply surviving in a concentration camp – no life, no dreams, no nothing. Dad was busy being a pastor, mom was depressed, and she was alone. There was nothing "really bad" that had happened to her, just a lack of anything good. She asked for nothing, wanted nothing and learned to depend on no one but herself for anything. The last I saw her, she had chosen drugs to help medicate her way though life. My heart cried as I saw her walk away from my office for the last time.

It all happens so gradually, so subtly, and more than likely, unintentionally. But it still happens, nonetheless. All the while it's applauded as spiritual servant hood, as "putting aside the flesh." While it may *look* like unselfish sacrifice to the casual observer, and even to your parents, it's not. I can kill you by shooting you with a gun. I can also kill you by starving you to death. The gun is noisy and noticeable. Starvation is silent and goes undetected, until it is too late. Either way, you end up dead.

One PK stated this so vividly when she said, "PKs are the sacrificial lambs on the altar of ministry." Sadly, she's often right.

"I'm Different"
CHAPTER 6

This heresy has nothing to do with the derogatory names your siblings or friends called you when you were growing up. This heresy has nothing to do with the legitimate "different-ness" MKs like me feel because of having a blended-culture thinking. I mean, how many other kids ride elephants to school every day so as not be attacked by lions! This is a great story African MKs have been known to tell to Sunday school classes while home on that thing called furlough. As an MK back in the States, I remember knowing I didn't fit in. I did the only thing I knew to do, try hard not to *stick out*. That is not the only thing that fuels this heresy.

The "I'm different" heresy comes from subtly being *treated* differently while you were growing up. You were under *different* rules. You had *different* expectations to live up to. These rules and expectations came from the forces of family and the church community. As much as church members may deny it, they *do* treat and judge the PK *differently*. It's an easy leap to make. "Since I have to *play* by different rules ... I must *be* different." Or "Since I have to *live up to* different expectations ... it must be because I *am* different. I have no idea why, I just am." This conclusion soon becomes your view of yourself.

The kernel of truth in all of this is that, as a PK, it's likely you did have different experiences and opportunities. You may have been able to travel more. You may have had the privilege of meeting the "big names" of the Christian faith or being around key leaders of the denomination. You may have been able to attend conferences, concerts, camps or mission trips that your peers only dreamed of attending. All these things are some of the "perks" of being the PK. Some of them are now priceless. Your experiences were different, that's true. But we are still members of the human race. The key is to separate the truth from the lie.

Another actual difference is the fact that you probably were exposed to different struggles in the life of the church or the denomination. You knew the financial problems of the church. You heard the bitter arguments over what color the carpet was to be in the new sanctuary. You knew which members were behind getting your father removed (kicked out is more like it). Maybe you wanted to know the inside scoop, maybe not, but you heard it anyway. And you were not free to tell anything to anyone. This too, makes you *different*.

While this heresy will not sink our boat by itself, it can still cause great injury. "I'm different" can keep you from pursuing friendships deeply, even today as an adult. It may give you that sense of uneasiness in social settings. It may keep you on edge when others are around. You may be overly sensitive to protocol and how you are not quite doing it right. You may be prone to isolate yourself because it's safer than feeling like you don't fit in. You may feel alone, even among friends. This tendency to isolate, mixed with feelings of loneliness, makes you susceptible to either depression or an inflated sense of what I call "stand-alone" arrogance. Both are internally damaging. "I'm different" can even interfere with your ability to sustain an intimate friendship with your spouse.

"I Can't Trust Anyone"
CHAPTER 7

You may be thinking, "Wait a minute. This isn't a heresy; it's the truth! I *know* what people are really like behind their Sunday faces. I *know* how loose people's tongues can be. I *know* how private confidences get passed around as 'prayer requests.' I *know* how often people, especially those in leadership positions, say one thing and live another. I *know* I can't trust anyone, ever!"

I have a hard time calling this one a heresy myself. The sad truth is that many people, even those within the stained glass reflections of the sanctuary, *cannot* be trusted. I am not trying to be cynical, just honest. Trust, loyalty and the discipline to keep that trust is not taught or modeled nearly enough these days. People's minds and tongues are lazy, sometimes even fickle, selfish and manipulative.

How many times have you shared or done something, only to have it end up as a sermon illustration? How many times have you shared with a teacher at the church-sponsored school, only to have it go to the principal, on to a church board member and finally end up, greatly altered of course, in your dad's study? How many times did you see your dad share a personal struggle in confidence, only to have it used against him at the next board meeting? How many times did you hear about the senior field missionary saying, "You can confide in me," only to find out it got all the way back to headquarters?

While stories like these are true, the "I can't trust *anyone*" still has enough fallacy in it to qualify as a heresy. Some people *cannot* be trusted. Period. It's foolish to try to trust them, whether they are believers or not. That may not sound Christian, but it is biblical. Check out Proverbs 25:19 sometime.

This lack of trust for legitimate reasons can easily make you cynical and sarcastic. Some people cannot even be trusted to believe the truth. Sarcasm is a safe medium for getting your message out. Chonda Pierce is a professional comedienne for a good reason. She knows she can say things as a comedienne that I couldn't say seriously. When you say it in a joke, you save yourself the time of reciting all the disclaimers. This cynical attitude is especially intense when talking about Christian leadership and authority in general. You spend a lot of your time trying to figure out what they really want. You wait for the other shoe to drop. You know it will. It's not a matter of if it will drop, just a question of when. So you wait.

But some people *are* trustworthy. They're not perfect, so their trustworthiness won't be perfect either. But you can find some people you can trust if you allow yourself the time to look. Without trust, there is no relationship. Without relationships, there is isolation. This isolation can cause depression, a common threat too many PKs, or it can mold you into an observer. You stand by and watch, but are never in the middle of the action. Just watching. To be the observer is safer. Your imperfections don't show. What they don't know yet stays hidden. No chinks in your armor will show. No weaknesses will be exposed for someone, someday to use against you.

David Gatewood gave me a vivid word picture of this when describing an experience he had. He remembers himself as a young boy peering out the window of his house in Switzerland at children playing out in the street. His little nose and hands were pressed against the glass, watching, not participating, not connected, just watching. When trust is absent, you end up like David, standing alone in silence, watching.

The other extreme of this same "I can't trust anybody" heresy is the urge to become the self-made, I'll-do-it-myself cynic who marches to his own drumbeat. You trust no one. You are driven. You spend too much time looking over your shoulder and checking the work of everyone else. You take no risks except the ones you can guarantee will turn out the way you want them to (not truly risks at all). And silently, anxiety rumbles through the gray matter of your brain. The cynicism and sarcasm grows; you may even cultivate it. You burn your bridges as quickly as you build them. And you find yourself alone.

During the time I have been writing this manuscript, I have become aware of my own lack of trust. It's not the cynical type, but the type that quietly says, "I walk alone. I will always walk alone." And I have. I do. My wife feels it. Others feel it too, I'm sure. I think alone, I write alone, I often climb the Colorado mountains alone. What I feel is not loneliness, it is alone-ness, unattached to anything or anyone. During our weekly Wednesday lunch together, David and I have been discussing the professional material on what is called Reactive Attachment Disorder. We see more and more of ourselves in these descriptions. We see more and more PKs and MKs who mirror the things we are feeling, but have never found the words to describe what they are feeling.

Not trusting anyone turns the world into a big, scary place. Your choices?

> Door # 1. Quit the world. Suicide sounds like the action of choice. If you choose not to slit your wrists, you may play Russian roulette with high risk

activities such as, but not limited to, rugby, drugs, sex, alcohol, etc.

You may not quit the whole world, but you may quit the church world. You walk out, shake the dust off of your sandals and never look back.

Door # 2. Build walls high enough and thick enough to keep the dangerous people from getting to your heart. Without trust, you walk alone. Maybe not socially, but certainly emotionally and maybe even spiritually. You can do this well because you have completed the "Christian Clichés 101" and "202" classes, with a 4.0 GPA no less! But you never share the real stuff of your heart. You learn not to need. Your heart's desire is *not* to desire. It's too risky. It makes you too vulnerable.

Door # 3. Sorry, you only have two options. Skip ahead to chapter ten if you want to understand why there are only two choices.

"I Can Ruin My Dad's Ministry"
CHAPTER 8

I cannot even begin to add up all the times that I have heard PKs and MKs tell me this one. The "I can ruin my dad's ministry" heresy can cause you to live in a state of constant mild anxiety. Fear of making one big mistake that will cost daddy his job. Fear that you will make one too many small mistakes that will remove dad from the pulpit.

I first met Amy Anders (not her real name) several years ago. Our paths have crossed on occasion through the years, and she recently shared this story with me:

> "I was in my early teen years, and my dad was thinking about taking a job at a new church. My sister had just had a very tumultuous year, and so everyone was a little on edge. My dad sat us down and said, 'Do you kids think you could behave well enough that I can take this job?' My translation – don't screw up, be perfect. You will ruin dad's ministry, thus ruining your welfare and his ability to provide for us. I was scared to death to look cross-eyed at *anyone* for fear of what would happen."

Sound familiar? To keep from ruining dad's precious ministry you try hard not to make any mistakes. That is, you try to be perfect. (Remember this one from chapter three?) You work overly hard to see that everyone is happy and comfortable, that other people's needs are met (cross-reference chapters five and nine). You become hyper-vigilant, overly sensitive to anything and everything that happens at the church. And if anything bad happens (usually at a rate of at least one time per week), you feel that it's your fault somehow. You feel responsible, even though you have no direct connection to the issue.

One of the big assumptions behind this heresy is that dad really *needs* this ministry, that he *has* to have it and therefore the whole family must guard it at all costs. Literally, at *all* costs. I have come to the conclusion that there are many people in ministry positions not because God called them there, but because their own inner wounds or needs or desires or selfishness drove them there. Maybe that's just my sarcasm coming out. Maybe it's a limited rat's-eye view of the chapel. Maybe it's the truth.

Another assumption that *sounds* logical is that *you* are the one ultimately responsible for seeing that dad keeps his position. After all (there are a lot of "after alls" in this book!), how can he rule the church if he can't maintain rule over his own house? *You* are the proof in his pudding. *You* make dad credible. *You* make him a genuine person and not a hypocrite. It's all on your grade school shoulders! Lucky you! Sure you can handle it; you're the preacher's kid.

Here enters a strange twist of human reality. Some parishioners *will* respond to your dad's sermon in direct proportion to how you sit in the pew. Some board members *will* reject your dad because of your unacceptable behavior. They did notice how fast you drove out of the parking lot after youth group last Wednesday. Your dad (more than likely, your mom) may have told you this word for word. Wow! What awesome power! A PK can totally dismantle the ministry of a forty-year-old, seminary-trained, six-foot-two man!

How overwhelming.

How empowering, though with a false sense of power.

How overbearing on your conscience.

How wrong!

Losing the pulpit or being de-credentialed by the denomination is between your dad, the congregation and the board or denomination leaders. But frequently one of these pulls you in, providing a "reason" for the actions being taken. This is the very fuel that keeps the "I can ruin my dad's ministry" heresy alive and well.

Believable, yes.

It's still a heresy, when compared with the truth.

"Other People's Needs Are More Important Than My Own"

CHAPTER 9

Oh, but of course! Everybody else's needs *are* more important than your own. Let me count the ways for you, in case you forgot:

- Dad's need for rest or quiet study time is more important than your need for math assistance or for playing football.

- The pew-sitters' needs for a "good example" to show their children is more important than your need to be treated like a normal child.

- The parishioner facing surgery takes precedence over the family vacation, never mind the fact that you haven't had one in three years, or that it has been planned for six months.

- Mom's need to look good and not be embarrassed is more important than your need to be a six-year-old kid (when you were six, that is).

- The building's need for new carpet is more important than your need for new school clothes.

- The denomination's need for a traveling youth speaker is more important than your need for a dad to tuck you in every night.

- The world's need for an evangelist is more important than your need for a dad.

Care to add any specific things to the list?

As if that's not bad enough, when you complained about it, some people, including your parents, called you selfish and immature. So you learned not to complain. You learned not to need. You slowly became anesthetized by the heresy and never woke up, emotionally, again.

David Gatewood tells of another time when his family lived in Germany right after World War II. They were living in a bombed out airport in Frankfurt (a very scary place for a child). The German government had given them a modular barrack and permission to stay at the airport site if they would take care of approximately ten to fifteen starving Nazi youth living among the rubble. To feed them, they began a garden. Gardens attract rabbits. They began raising rabbits for food too. One of the German boys gave David a bunny to keep as his own. As time passed, his bunny became the biggest of the lot. The image is still pressed into his memory of coming home one day and finding the rabbit skin of *his* bunny hanging on the side of the cage. The words of his dad still ring in his mind: "Well, son, *they* needed the food. This is your way of giving to the Lord's work." No acknowledgment of the shock or pain David felt, no opportunity to share the feelings openly. The message was clear, "Others' needs are more important than your own."

It's so easy for parents, church leaders and members of the congregation to assume you will simply surrender your needs "for the good of the ministry." They also assume that it's the *right* thing for you to do. True, some crises cannot be avoided or planned around. Sometimes your plans have to be altered or set aside. Usually the smaller the church the more this tends to happen. But when that becomes the pattern, the heresy takes root in fertile ground. Once the roots have a firm grip, the heresy becomes a record in the jukebox of your mind to be played over and over again.

A single heresy rarely stands alone. The vines of several heresies intertwine to team up against your mind and heart: "I have to be perfect" and therefore shouldn't have needs. "I should already know" how to handle my problems and *not* be so needy anyway. Having needs is a sign of weakness or spiritual immaturity. And if any of this gets out, it may "ruin my dad's ministry." So there you are, "damned if you do and damned if you don't". By the way, that's a whole heresy in itself, coming up in the next chapter.

Sometimes the combination of heresies can literally kill the soul. Amy told me of a time she and a boy were in a sexual situation that was way out of her control. After the ordeal, she found out that someone else had been watching the entire encounter and proceeded to blackmail her. Amy was so afraid of saying anything to anyone because she would "ruin her dad's ministry," and because she was not "perfect." This continued for a long period of time. She gave what he demanded (sex) and he blackmailed her for more. "I killed myself," she said, "my longings, me, my feelings, to protect my family and everyone in the church." Here is a girl who allowed herself to be sexually violated, all because she believed other people's needs for her to put on a good appearance were more important than her *own* need for safety and sanity. Amy is not alone. These heresies are not mere semantics. They are real and they can really hurt.

"Other people's needs are more important than my own" is a heresy often preached from the pulpit, maybe even by your own dad. But it's still a heresy, in spite of the fact that there may be three points, an acrostic, an illustration and a Scripture reference thrown in from time to time. Syrup of Ipecac doesn't magically change when you change the label to read "flavored cough syrup." I dare you to try it sometime! Slapping a Bible verse onto this heresy does not make it anything different than what it is – a heresy. The truth may be close, but not in this bottle.

I remember the story of the five-year old pastor's daughter who was the only child in the church's kindergarten classroom made to share her lunch with the one student who had forgotten hers. Like this daughter, we were often sacrificed on the altar of ministry. And being sacrificed hurts! Especially when we were given no choice on the matter.

There's a huge difference between surrendering to the will of God and being sacrificed for the sake of the ministry. Surrendering is personal, between God and you, and you come to the point where you take a knee and give yourself over to His control. That's good, that's right … but that's not what this heresy does. This heresy has the aroma of being sold into slavery … something against your will and without your consent. That's where the "being sacrificed" takes place.

Surrender is good.

Slavery and sacrifice is just plain wrong.

Think about it, were you sold into "servanthood"?

"I'm Damned If I Do and Damned If I Don't"
CHAPTER 10

While most of the heresies listed in this book are lies with some truth in them, this statement is mostly true with just a bit of a lie in it. Think back. Many times you were placed in an either/or situation.

EITHER you are a goodie-two-shoes,
OR you're the town rebel.

EITHER you agree with everything dad says and does,
OR you're perceived to be against all that he stands for.

EITHER you are a servant,
OR they call you selfish.

EITHER it's a rock,
OR it's a hard place. (Just seeing if you're reading carefully!)

EITHER you totally agree with everything the mission does,
OR you are anti-missions.

You are forced to live an either/or existence. Since you see more of the inside workings of the ministry, since you see the gap between what leaders say and how they live, since you know what people are *really* like, you are in a bind. A double-bind. Double-bind is a technical term used to describe a situation where you are faced with two conflicting messages. Regardless of which one you heed, you disregard the other and lose. Herein is the "Damned if I do and damned if I don't." For some of you with strong denominational ties, or sensitive ears, it's "Darned if I do and darned if I don't."

Either ...

... you will pretend that things are fine and wonderful when you know differently. You do your part to pretend that all the leadership is fine, upstanding Christian servants and that your family is the shining example of what a Christian family should be. You get stereotyped as a goodie-two-shoe, a.k.a. "a servant."

The problem with this option is that it's wrong, and you know it. Everything is *not* fine. The leadership is *not* perfect and always above reproach. Things are *not* comfortable and nice all the time. You *don't* like living in a small town. You *don't* like living in the city. You do *not* agree that living with dad is like living with God, even if other people think so. You *are* lonely. You *do* have hurts and fears. But you are bound by a vow of silence, and the incongruence builds inside, along with tension, frustration, unmet needs, anger, anxiety and loneliness.

The inside pressure builds until it erupts. You can only pretend for so long. You can only keep the frustration bottled up for so long. It may come out violently. More than likely, if you choose this option, it will come out in subtle ways.

You may turn to food to either punish or medicate yourself. You try to relieve the anxiety or the tension by eating. You use food to cope. The actual dynamics of eating disorders plays out in one of three ways:

(1)   Overweight or obesity. You eat to ease the anxiety. You eat to soothe the pain. You eat to not feel so lonely. You eat as a way of turning the anger onto yourself. Food becomes a friend that is always there for you. It never rejects or rebukes you. Food can be a way to medicate the pain or the anger.

(2)   Bulimia or binge-and-purge. You eat for the same reasons stated above, with the added action of making it all come up again. That way you have the comfort of the food without the weight gain. That way, no one can see anything "unacceptable" at all.

(3)   Anorexia. You keep from eating and gaining weight as the ultimate way to gain some control over your out-of-control life. Add the obsession our culture has with being thin to the pressures and anxieties that come with the glass house, and you have the lethal emotional mixture necessary for anorexia.

Back to Amy. The pressure to be perfect, combined with the emotional pain of being sexually exploited, trying to keep a secret, and the constant presence of blackmail hanging overhead finally got to her. Is it any wonder she couldn't pretend anymore? Is it a surprise that survival kicked in and she grasped wildly at anything that would offer a feeling of control? Food was what she grabbed on to. *No one* could force her to eat. *No one* could control that one aspect of her life. It was totally in *her* control. "It was mine. All mine," she said.

If you can't physically escape the tyranny of the double-bind, you may try to escape *mentally*. You "check out." You lose yourself in daydreams, music or novels. Maybe not on purpose, but you escape inside your mind to a world of fantasy. The reasoning behind all this is quite simple. If you cannot *deal* with the pressures and pains of the real world, and you cannot *escape* them, you are left with only one choice – create a pretend world where the pressures and pain can be ignored. You create a mental oasis, a time-out, a safe place. Or you may simply become numb. You don't go off to a fantasy world; you just disappear into a big black hole of nothingness.

Escaping is not bad in and of itself (just not while you're driving). Escape becomes damaging when you spend more time escaping than living. It becomes damaging when it interferes with the real world of work, school, relationships or personal motivation.

The fantasy becomes dangerous, and wrong, when it evolves into some kind of sexual fantasy such as pornography (hard or soft), voyeurism, affairs or a host of other sexual dysfunctions. I talked with Dr. Harry Schaumburg, author of *False Intimacy*, who has been working with sexual addictions for the past 18 years. He is a former missionary to Afghanistan who currently works with many Christian leaders struggling with sexual addictions of various kinds. He said that it's easy to progress from a benign fantasy world into a sexual fantasy world. After all, we are sexual beings. The combination of pressures, expectations, the image of being the "healer," and the strange isolationism ("I'm different") inherent to the job puts pastors, particularly, at risk. "It's an occupational hazard," he says. "It's just my educated guess, but I think PKs are more prone to be susceptible to pornography than the normal kid." It makes sense. If the pressures and pain can lead an adult pastor to create a sexual escape, how much more can those pressures, expectations, and pains suck the pastor's son into an unhealthy sexual escape?

DID YOU KNOW: In a 1991 Survey of Pastors, 80 percent of practicing pastors thought ministry negatively affects them or their family.[1]

If the pastor's daughter can keep her eating disorder well hidden, so too, the preacher's son can keep his sexual fantasy hidden. Thanks to the internet and "900" telephone numbers, you can access anything you want, and even things you *don't* want, in the privacy of your own home or office. No one will know – not the congregation, not your employer, not your family, not even your spouse. And it's a pathway to destruction. While I want to acknowledge that there are other contributing factors that lure men into sexual fantasies and addictions, behind it all is an urge to escape: the pain, isolationism, or something else entirely.

These are the "either" choices. Any one you choose, you lose.

Or ...

... you speak up. You go your own way. In an attempt to break the goody-two-shoes stereotype, you try to be your own person only to find out you ended up in another stereotype, the town rebel. I can hear it now.

"Well, you know Mabel; he's the preacher's son."

"No wonder he acts so uncontrollable, Thelma."

"Umm, yes well, I pity his mother. Sweet lady, she is."

You jump out of the frying pan and land in the fire, from one bad label to another. You just cannot win for losing! Even if you *wanted* to do the right thing, even if you *wanted* to be in the choir, people will think you are there just because you are the preacher's kid. You get no credit for yourself. Even if you *wanted* to go your own way, even if you *wanted* to be your own person, people will still think you are rebelling just because you are the preacher's kid. You *still* get no credit.

"I can't win. I just can't win!"

If you live with this long enough, it will mold your perceptions so that you only see in black and white …

- Accept or reject.
- Win or lose.
- Love all or hate everything.
- Succeed or fail.
- Good or bad.
- Perfect or failure.
- Angel or demon.

There's no middle ground. No "*and*" to bring a balance or reality into your worldview. This is the exact dynamic that trapped Janie, the MK from the Far East, back in chapter one. The mission agency, missionary friends and even her parents had trapped her in a double-bind. If she ever spoke up, she was unofficially reprimanded and rebuked. If she kept quiet, she silently self-destructed from the inside out. Either way, she lost.

I have talked about sarcasm in earlier chapters. (You may have noticed a bit of it throughout these pages too.) The genesis of sarcasm springs out of the very middle of the double-bind. Since telling the truth is not allowed and keeping silent is not totally possible, you cloak the truth in sarcasm. If you are unable to beat up the playground bully, you spit in his milk carton when he looks away! The behavior is called passive-aggressive. Sarcasm is the passive-aggressive behavior in words. At least you can get some of the information out and feel partially vindicated. It becomes a coping mechanism, a survival tactic, an attempt to get out of the double-bind that you find yourself in time and again.

Notes

1. 1991 Survey of Pastors, Fuller Institute of Church Growth, as cited by H.B. London, Jr. and Neil B. Wiseman, *Pastors at Risk*, (Wheaton, IL: Victor Books, 1993), 30.

"God Is Disappointed With Me"
CHAPTER 11

One logical conclusion, after all these heresies have played in your mind for so long, is the obvious "God is disappointed with me." Of course, because:

- You're *not* perfect.
- You *don't* already know the things you *should* know.
- You *do* have doubts.
- You're *not* far enough along in your spiritual journey or faith.
- You *are* angry with God sometimes.
- You *are* sarcastic about church leadership.
- You *do* have needs and want them met.
- You *don't* always put other's needs ahead of your own.
- You *do* lack trust, but you *should* trust.
- You see all the ways you have "hindered" dad's ministry, and therefore, God's ministry.
- You pretend, while knowing that God hates hypocrisy.

"A holy, pure, righteous, just God would *have* to be disappointed with me." Or so your jukebox says. I worked with one PK in my counseling practice who was literally terrified of God. She was afraid He would "zap" her for any little thing that was not exactly perfect. Worse yet, God would "zap" her for being a "bad girl." At least that's how she saw herself. She kept doing the right spiritual things, attending church, studying the Bible ... all that stuff. What she did *not* do was draw close to the person of God, or allow Him to come close to her. She is not alone by any stretch of the imagination.

Amid fear and worry, you, like she, may still do the right things. Theologically, you know that God is not the problem here, so it *must* be you. You simply lack the effort. You are slack in your discipline. Your faith is weak. So you try harder and harder to make God pleased with you. You try to make Him happy and comfortable just as you spend your life trying to make *people* happy and comfortable.

You keep busy in an attempt to stay one step ahead of the self-contempt and out-of-control feelings that nip at your heels. You may even develop obsessive-compulsive behaviors and thinking patterns.

Trying ...

Trying ...

Trying to do enough to make God pleased
and no longer disappointed with you.

PKs are "s-m-a-r-t." If this is your view of God, you know better than to let Him come close to your heart. You will do what you can to keep what you feel will be a safe distance from Him. You may decide to dump God all together. Dump the baby (God) out with the bath water (church politics). No more pretending. No more living the way *they* expect you to. No more interest in trusting God. No more spiritual life inside either. You walk out the sacred doors and never look back. Your record is not "God is disappointed with me," but rather, "God is a disappointment *to* me." How can He call Himself righteous and tolerate all the junk you saw going on behind the scenes?

How can He say He cares, then not put an end to the abuse you received at the hands of pastor dad?

How can He say He controls everything when He didn't even intervene to stop the sexual molestation that traumatized you?

How could He?

You concluded either that His hands were tied, or that He really could care less about you.

You don't care any longer, anyway … either.

You know all the church clichés. They are too shallow to answer the questions you are really asking. "So," you say to yourself, "why try anymore?" You walk away from the organized church, and from God, too.

Whether you keep running on the hamster's spinning wheel, or if you choose to walk away, you are the one who loses. You still end up dead and empty, spiritually. Whether you even care anymore or not, you still walk around with a hurting, wounded heart. Either way, the heresy wins and you lose. "So what else is new?" a voice whispers. "It's always been that way."

If the stories I have shared in the last nine chapters seem extreme to you, count your blessings! Be aware that mild experiences, as well as the traumatic ones, can breed these holy heresies. If your life's history makes a horror movie look like a "Leave It To

Beaver" episode, I *am* sorry. I have purposefully refrained from sharing more traumatic stories than these in order to sidestep any accusations of trying to be sensational. I have quite literally heard it all. Whatever mixture of good and bad you experienced as a PK, I hope you can benefit from some of what has been shared.

PART III:

WHAT'S THE SOLUTION … HONESTLY, NOW?

HONEST PAIN … HONEST HEALING

Assessing the Damage

The first step in any healing process is evaluating the situation, taking stock of what is wrong and determining how it can be remedied. If you have not already done so, give yourself official permission *to* think, *to* feel and *to* talk. Listen to the other side of the *and* in the sentence. Listen past the pat answers. My hope is that you have been doing this while reading.

> **FROSTBITE:** Healing the wounded-ness of your heart is a lot like the frostbite I experienced after one particularly challenging and dangerous climb. As long as you are numb, you feel no pain. All feels fine. Denial works, and works well. At least you don't *feel* any pain. That's why we use it. That's not to say that all really *is* well; you just can't feel the brokenness. Just like my fingers. When they were frozen, I felt no pain and could handle cuts and falling rocks without even a flinch. But the freeze was still working its damage. When I began to thaw my hands and feet in the bathtub, in the safety of my home, whoa Nellie! I began to feel the pain, intensely and deeply. Here is why people choose to stay numb and in denial – it hurts too much to see clearly. It hurts too much to thaw out. I wish there was an easier way, but the only way to

healing is *through* the pain.

Now, time for your check-up. Let's see how many of the heresies have infiltrated your thinking. Let's see if there is some numbness or frostbite in your heart. I have summarized the nine holy heresy statements on the next two pages. Mark how accurately they describe your thinking, whether verbalized aloud or not. Mark the highest number that describes how you either think now, or have thought in the past.

(on the next few pages are some
tests and surveys you may find helpful)

THE HOLY HERESIES THAT PK/MKs OFTEN DEVELOP

Make your marks using this scale:

> 1 = Not true at all
> 2 = Somewhat true
> 3 = Mostly true
> 4 = Almost always true

1 2 3 4   1) **"I HAVE TO BE PERFECT."** I feel (or was told) that "image is everything." I was held up as an example for others to follow.

1 2 3 4   2) **"I SHOULD ALREADY KNOW."** I feel I was born mature and that I *should* be farther along than I am right now.

1 2 3 4   3) **"I'M HERE FOR OTHERS."** It seems my job is to make other people comfortable.

1 2 3 4   4) **"I'M DIFFERENT."** I seem to live with a different set of expectations and rules than others.

1 2 3 4   5) **"I CAN'T TRUST ANYONE."** I *know* what people and churches are *really* like under the surface and I don't trust them.

1 2 3 4   6) **"I CAN RUIN MY DAD'S MINISTRY."** I have been told this or felt it often.

1 2 3 4   7) **"OTHER PEOPLE'S NEEDS ARE MORE IMPORTANT THAN MY OWN."** I often think that

my needs are less important than others' needs. I feel that others are hurting more than I am and they need dad's, or God's, time and energy more than I do.

1 2 3 4   8) **"I'M DAMNED IF I DO AND DAMNED IF I DON'T."** I feel stuck. There is no middle ground. I feel that I have to go along with everything or I am anti-ministry. I find myself to be sarcastic and cynical.

1 2 3 4   9) **"GOD IS DISAPPOINTED WITH ME."** I am not perfect and I feel I should be. I feel that I am living a lie by pretending, and I know God hates lies and pretending. I would get angry at Him too, but that's not allowed. Sometimes I feel as if He hates me because I often feel I am "bad."

IMPACTING FORCES ON PK/MKs

Complete the worksheet below. How would you rate these forces on your life? What percentage would you assign to each of the categories in the left-hand column in terms of their relative impact on your life? The "Other" is a catch-all category in case something doesn't fit into the big three. The four numbers on the left will total 100 when you're through. Then take the percentages from the left in each category and distribute the total into what you would describe as "good" impact or "bad" impact. The two numbers (good plus bad) need to total the corresponding number immediately to their left. Be a good little kid and tell the truth now!

[   ] **FAMILY**   [   ] The good [   ] The bad

[   ] **CHRISTIAN**   [   ] The good [   ] The bad
    COMMUNITY

[   ] **CULTURE (S)**   [   ] The good [   ] The bad

[   ] **OTHER STUFF**   [   ] The good [   ] The bad

_____

100%

SIDE NOTE (I like these diversions!): In the research I have been doing on PKs and these forces of impact, most PKs have rated their families and church communities as mostly having good impact. That sounds fine and dandy (Professional research terms, you know!) but those same respondents also showed signs of the holy heresies in their belief system. A rocket scientist I am not, but something doesn't add up here. How could everything be fine environmentally and the PK still end up mentally and emotionally wounded and bruised? How could all the music of life have been fine, yet they still come out with warped records? Not all of this can be blamed on the culture ("the world" as it's often called from the pulpit). Are they still keeping secrets? Is it a conditioned response? Is it the "right" answer they gave without thinking? I don't know yet.

Did you pass or fail? Just kidding! There is no "failing," just a scoring grid to help you decide what action to take based on your above responses.

Add up the nine numbers you circled to the left of each of the statements

For every "3" you circled, add 2 extra points 2 X _____ = _____

For every "4" you circled, add 5 extra points 5 X _____ = _____

TOTAL OF ALL POINTS   = _____

Note each of the "3" and "4" responses you circled. You need to work individually on each of these heresies, regardless of your TOTAL score and category listed below.

If your TOTAL score was between 9 and 18: your overall jukebox is in pretty good shape. Go pick flowers or blow up a balloon and give it to somebody. Assuming you were honest with yourself, you have weathered the occupational hazards of being a PK well. You have a lot to be thankful for.

If your TOTAL score was between 19 and 27: you have some warped records that need serious attention. Look into those faulty conclusions and how to correct them with the truth. Reading self-help books and keeping a journal are good first steps. Still pick the flowers, but leave the balloon alone until the reading is done. See the suggested reading list in the Appendix. Talking with a trusted friend may prove to be very beneficial as well.

If your TOTAL score was between 28 and 44: you are in need of outside assistance. The reading and journaling will help, but since the heresies are deep and pervasive, you will need the help of a wise and trusted friend who can assist you both in finding the truth and reminding you of it. If you still want to pick flowers, go ahead. But be thinking, reading, journaling and talking as you pick.

If your TOTAL score was between 45 and 81: you need to seek professional help. You're in serious trouble, even if it doesn't feel like it. Forget picking flowers, spend your time picking a good counselor. The reading, journaling and talking to a friend is not going to be enough to bind up all the broken pieces. Put the balloon in your pocket. It will be a good reminder that all of life is not work and healing!

Since were doing assessments here, let me make a few comments regarding this thing called depression. The "D" word has popped up fairly regularly to this point hasn't it? Ok ... First of all, it is a real disorder. It's not just "all in your head" as some say. Second, it's not "fixed" by praying and reading your bible more. Depression is a genuine biological and psychological disorder (see first point again) that likely will need biological and psychological interventions. If you are truly depressed, you can't "pull yourself out of it." You just can't. It won't work and you'll feel guilty for failing to "dig yourself out of the hole you're in." Instead, seek professional help and if medication is needed ... take it ... and don't feel guilty. You may not tell everybody else you're on antidepressants, but they don't need to know anyway.

If you care to help me out with the ongoing survey I'm working on, fill out the demographic information below. Email your responses or reactions on the Holy Heresies and Impacting Forces, along with the Demographic Stuff to:

> Timothy L. Sanford, M.A.
> c/o LifEdvice: info@lifedvice.com

THE DEMOGRAPHIC STUFF

Check one: ___PK ___MK ___Parachurch-Kid

Age: _____ Age when your parents began ministry _____

Number of years as a PK/MK _____ Male / Female (Circle one)

Age when you **left home** or your parents ended ministry _____

Number of siblings _____ Your place in the birth order _____

Are you in ministry now? ___ Yes ___ No

PLEASE HELP: There is an extra survey in the Appendix. Make copies of it and pass it along to any and all adult PK/MKs you know. While this survey was never intended to be an official piece of research, it is helping those of us who are working with PK/MKs.

You can also use this extra survey for yourself ... in case you didn't fill yours out *perfectly*! "Neatness is next to godliness!" they always say.

FOR THE CURIOUS: How "normal" are you? I have been collecting research since 1997 and have received responses from all over the world (literally, all six inhabited continents). Here are the ongoing survey results:

29% of all responses were marked "Almost always true."

20% of all responses were marked "Mostly true."

That makes 49% of all responses marked either "Almost always true" or "Mostly true." That's a lot, folks!

24% of the people who responded to the survey had more than five "Almost always true" responses. This means that *more than half* of the holy heresies are present in their jukeboxes at a deep and powerful level.

42% of the people who responded to the survey are now in ministry. I guess it's hard to leave the rat race, isn't it?

In contrast to the noticeable presence of heresies in the thinking of those responding, the survey pool reported that:

74% of the family's impact was positive, the "good."
59% of the church community's impact was positive (not that great of a percentage, is it?).
61% of the culture's impact was positive.

Something does *not* add up here. How can 49% of the responses be marked "Almost always true" or "Mostly true," when 66% of all the impact was marked "good"? What is wrong with this picture? My guess is that (1) the forces of family, community and culture play a much bigger part in our lives than we realize and (2) there *was* more "bad" impact than what we want to, dare to, or *know how to* see. This pattern has been consistent from the outset.

At this point, you have some choices to make based upon the quiz results in front of you. If you need to make some changes, there's no better time to begin than right now.

Lesson number one is one I learned many years ago on the high school football field. I believe it's a lesson that would be very fitting here too: pain is *not* the enemy.

I do not *like* pain. I do *not* go looking for it. But it is *not* the enemy, either. It is *not* to be avoided *at all costs*. Believe me, I avoid it when I can! But sometimes what I want and need is on the other side of the pain. To get there, I will have to feel the pain for a while.

The old maxims my coaches shouted at me (while I was dying during wind sprints!) come back to haunt me.

"No pain, no gain!"

"No grunt, no grow!"

I hated them for saying those things! Especially as they stood there sipping cool lemonade and chewing on sunflower seeds! There is truth here, even when you are off the practice field.

One PK who was seeing me at my private practice offered to buy a sign for my door that read "Torture Chamber." It has a strong hint of the truth to it, but it would be terrible for my image and not very good for business. Pain is *not* the enemy; ignorance, denial and worry are.

Let the Journey Continue
CHAPTER 13

The journey continues because, if you're still with me, you're already on your way out of the rat maze. The healing and maturing process is not as simple as constructing a Sunday morning sermon: Introductory story, three main points, an illustration, altar call and a closing prayer, it does however, follow a pattern.

(1) You *become aware* of each faulty conclusion you have been living under – the holy heresies or others.

(2) You *call it what it is*, a lie. You admit the error or partial error in your thinking. You admit you have a warped record or two.

(3) Then you *go searching for what the truth is*, that which *is* more accurate than the conclusion you now hold on to as true.

(4) Once you have found something more accurate and true, you *make a new recording*. You establish a new belief statement to address the subject at hand.

(5)   Lastly, you *do the change out*.   With discipline and determination, (maybe even the help of a friend or therapist) you engage in the hard mental process of stopping the old record from playing while starting up the new one.

Become aware of possible faulty conclusions

The biggest hurdle to surmount is the lack of awareness. You have no way of evaluating or changing anything you don't even know exists. If you were to get into a street fight with a blindfold on, you would surely lose. I know too, it takes a willingness to have conclusions that have been with you for so long opened up to scrutiny. As you look, you will discover that many of your conclusions *are* accurate and good. Great! Keep them. If your car has a shimmy in the front end, you wouldn't scrap the entire vehicle. You have a good vehicle, with a small alignment problem. Keep the car, fix the alignment and go on your way again. The same is true when looking at your thinking patterns. Keep all the good things, the good records, the good conclusions you have drawn, and fix up the things that need work.

A common oversight when looking at your past and present is to focus all your attention on whatever bad happened to cause the pain and faulty thinking. Faulty conclusions *do* come from the pain of bad experiences. They *also* come from experiences where good things did *not* happen. Remember, as we saw back in chapter five, I can kill you with a gun (doing a "bad" thing). I can also starve you to death (*not* doing a "good" thing). Be aware of the presence of damaging experiences, as well as the absence of nurturing ones.

Call it what it is

If the records in your jukebox are accurate and true, great! Polish them up, put them back in and listen to the music. If a record or two is warped, say so. When you finally admit what the truth is, you become free to grow and make the changes needed. Almost sounds biblical huh – "Then you will know the truth, and the truth will set you free" (John 8:32). Denial (not the river in Egypt) is the therapeutic term for refusing to call a spade a spade. Denial means you are aware that something is wrong (stage one), but you refuse to acknowledge its existence.

Search for what is true and accurate

This is the Research & Development Department of the process. The more time you spend in the parsonage, or on the field, the more you know all the clichés and answers. But what is the *truth*? What *is* a more accurate conclusion to the matter? What really *is* true, whether it feels like it or not?

At this stage of the journey, you need outside input. You need to know more than you know. Read. Talk with others you respect and trust. Ask questions. Test what you hear. Test what you have believed for so many years. Does it work in the real world? Is it consistent? Is it *always* true? Yes, and go back to the Scriptures to see if the memory verses you got all those stars for are indeed true and interpreted accurately.

Make a new recording

Take the new data and formulate a short statement. Cut a "new release" recording. Write it down in your own words, words that make sense to you. Put it on a card and carry it with you if you need to. I have personalized many Scripture verses, as if God himself is speaking directly to me and with my actual circumstances in mind. Somehow I need a way for the words to move off the onion-skin paper and into flesh and blood. As I have done this with verses over the years, it has made the personal relationship with God more personal, and more of a relationship. What a concept!

Do the change out

You will find that old records die hard, even though you now can tell the lie from the truth. The longer you have lived by the old records, the longer it will take to re-tune your ear to the truth. Over the years, your jukebox has adjusted to the warped records. So too, your behavior has adjusted to the presence of the heresies. It will take time and energy for things to move back into a balanced place. Be patient and stubborn. Stubbornness is good in this case. It will help you get through the awkward period of change. Your mind will still default to the old records, the old conclusions, the old emotions. It's a habit. It's familiar. It's "family" to your thinking. You can run the old rat maze blindfolded, with one foot tied behind your back, and still make record time! Now the maze is changed and you have to think. Now you have to do it differently. Now you need to change. With the new record of the truth, you will have to consciously choose to make the change from the old to the new, at least for a while.

I have never liked being late. I hate being late to anything. This is a strange twist for someone who was raised in a Latin culture! Several years ago, I became aware of the record behind why I hate to be late. I held to the conclusion that "competent people are never late." It sounded good to me. If you really *were* competent, you would have factored in enough time to get there on time. Right? Makes sense to me! Being competent was the same as being perfect. It took several weeks for this record to become clear enough for me to call it what it was. It is close to the truth, but not quite. At this point, I had to rethink my definition of competency. I had to search for a more accurate definition of what being competent really looked like. It's not based on punctuality. I know people who are on time to everything, but are not very competent. I also know very competent people who are sometimes late. I had to make a new recording that went something like this; "I am a competent person even though I may arrive late." It sounded meaningless at the start, but over time it proved truer than the old recording. Slowly the change out occurred in my thinking. I still strive to be on time, but I don't beat up on myself if I get there a bit late. I also am more tolerant of others when they are late.

It is estimated that it takes thirty days to form a new habit. It makes sense that it takes longer to *break* one. With breaking away from the old conclusions and focusing on the new ones, you are looking at a minimum of two to four months' time. At some point though, the new records will become the automatic ones, the default, finally. Honest, it will happen. As this happens, you really do become free. You may or may not notice the shift, but it will come. Be patient. Be stubborn. As the old warped records (the heresies) get destroyed and replaced by the new releases (the truth), it will be music to your ears!

> "Say, while you're in there, change the needle too, will ya?"

The following chapters deal with specific areas of the healing journey that befall many PKs in their quest for health and freedom from the heresies. The issues of perfectionism, anxiety, forgiveness, trust and an honest pursuit of God, are not unique to PKs, but PKs are the ones who are not allowed to struggle with these issues. Besides, why would *you* need to struggle? Didn't you live in the most godly house in town? Don't you have an inside line to God? Surely *you* shouldn't struggle with anything.

> "Enough, already, Elmer!"

Dealing With the Tyrant "Shoulds"
CHAPTER 14

Perfectionism is subtler than merely having to have everything "just so." Whether you are a perfectionist or not is not always decided by the order of your closet. Perfectionistic thinking is not solely based upon how perfect you want things to be, but on how you think they *should* be. Perfectionism is, in part, deep-seated thinking patterns (remember the jukebox word picture?) that hold onto a concise, rigid view of how things *should* be done in order to be done *right*. There is *one* way to do something and you *should* do it that way.

Why?

"Because that's the *right way* to do it."

Who said?

"*They* did …

… and I *shouldn't* question them."

The *should* phrases have permeated this book, mainly because it permeates so many PKs' jukeboxes. It's dangerous thinking. I would be safe in guessing that the more *should* records you have, the more anxious, angry and/or depressed you are. Why? For several reasons.

No options

Should thinking leaves you with no viable options. You do it the way you *should*, or you're wrong. You failed. It's either/or for you. If you do each thing the way you *should*, you succeed. And after all, you *should* do it the *should* way.

If you do it any other way,

you've failed,

which makes you a failure ... and a jerk.

With the *should* recording, you have no real options.

No choice

If you have no options, it follows suit that you have no choices. You *have* to do it the way you *should*. You simply *have* to.

- You *have* to like church, because you *should* like it.
- You *have* to be full of smiles, because you *should* be "living victoriously."

No options, no choice. You are a mere serf to a tyrant that is invisibly lording over and shaking a religious pseudo-god finger at you.

- "You *should* have been nicer to her."
- "You *shouldn't* be so angry at God!"

- "You *should* be more mature."
- "You *shouldn't* struggle with the hard things you grew up with."
- "They *should* just get over it and grow up."
- "You *shouldn't* need help."
- "You *should* be stronger."

Condemnation and fear

Tyrants impose submission by using condemnation and fear. The *shoulds* do no less. Every one of the statements listed above is only half-complete. The part listed is what you may hear and/or say. The second half is rarely verbalized, but is present nonetheless. Listen to some of them again.

- "You *have* to love all people ...
                    but you *don't* ... jerk!"

- "You *shouldn't* be so angry at God ...
                    but you *are* ... heathen, sinner, scumbag!"

- "You *shouldn't* struggle with the hard things you grew up with ...
                    but you *do* ... blamer."

- "They *should* just get over it and grow up ...
                    but they *won't* ... babies!"

- "You *shouldn't* need help. You *should* be stronger ...
                    but you *do*, and you *aren't* ... lazy, wimp!"

CONFRONTATION: By the way, who made *you* God? Who made *them* God? Who gave either of you the power to decide what *should* be done, *should* be said or *should* be followed? How did *you* get to know it all and decide what is the one *right way* to do everything? Who made *you* God? Who made *them* God?

Anywhere there is a *should*, there is a judgment, an indictment at the end. If you live with the tyrant of the *shoulds*, you will become an expert at self-contempt. If you place others under the same yoke of *should* thinking; you will boil with contempt for others. Even if the contempt doesn't come out our mouth.

If you have to act the exact way you *should*, you run a high risk of *not* performing exactly the *right* way, every time, with everything. Most of your choices, then, become a showdown between succeed or fail, win or lose, live or die, *should* or sin. That high probability if imperfection is the spawning ground for anxiety and worry.

"I *should* be nicer."

"But, *what if* I'm not?"

"*What if* I really don't care about them?"

"But I *should*."

"But, *what if* I really don't care?"

"*What if* God is hearing all of this?"

"*What if* He hates me for thinking this way?"

"What if ..."

Breaking the anxious *what if* thinking will be covered in the next chapter, but here you need to purge your jukebox of the *should* conclusions. The *shoulds* that sound so spiritual but are not.

But they *sound* good. They *sound* true.

They're *not* accurate.

But they *should* be accurate, *shouldn't* they? After all, I got them right out of the Bible. Didn't I?

I do *not* believe that everything is relative and up for debate based on personal conclusions. I am *not* saying that it is healthy to "believe what you want to believe, just as long as you're sincere." (More disclaimers to keep the theologians among us content.) The Scriptures are clear. There are "thou shalt" and "thou shalt not" statements. There are key issues that are make-no-apologies-about-it right or wrong. But God has never forced mankind, or any individual, into obedience. God has never chosen for people. He did not choose for Adam and Eve; He does not choose for you. God lays out the right and the wrong. He lays out the consequences and the rewards for each. He clearly encourages you to choose the right way. But He never overrides your will or manipulates you into behaving a certain way.

"Well there, Mr. Sanford, I believe in predestination. I believe it's God who chooses."

"Predestination my foot! We choose God. He doesn't choose us. Isn't that true, Mr. Author, Sir?"

"Oh, leave him alone, he's not talking about 'saving

faith,' he's talking about the way we live our everyday lives!"

The book of Proverbs is clear in stating the ways of wisdom. Solomon also makes no bones about the responsibility of choosing. Some will choose wisdom, some foolishness.

"But we *should* choose right, *shouldn''t* we?"

"If we want to call ourselves Christians, we *have* to choose wisdom, right?"

"I'm lost!"

If the *should* thinking pattern is inaccurate, what is better? What is more accurate and true?

"I think he *should* explain things better, Rudy. He *shouldn't* try to confuse us so."

"You're right, Bonnie. He'll *have* to make more sense than this if he wants to convince me of how I *should* change my thinking!"

I hope from all of this that you can begin to hear the way the *should* thinking forms. It's subtle, and often is such a part of your thinking that you don't even realize its presence. The *should* thinking is dangerous, though. Whether or not you're convinced yet, read on. Tyrants don't just surrender. Some tyrants exert much energy attempting to convince the serfs of their utter dependence on them. But the *shoulds* can be changed for the better. Once again, it's a matter of exchanging the lie for the truth.

- THE LIE: "I *should* ..."

- THE TRUTH: "I *could* ..."
                 "I *would like* ..."
                       "I *choose to* ..."

Before you think I'm simply playing a stupid psycho word-game, check it out. See if it fits the statements listed earlier. See if the statements remain true. See if the *coulds* are more accurate than the *shoulds*.

> THE LIE: "You *shouldn't* be so angry at God ...
>   but you *are* ... heathen, sinner, scumbag!"

> THE TRUTH: "I *could* be angry at God, if I wanted to ...
>   I *wish* I wasn't."

It's true you *could* be angry with God. You *are* angry, and still alive too! You *can* be angry. You may still *want* to be angry, yet *wish* you weren't. The option is yours, the choice is yours, *without* the self-contempt or condemnation from God. Take a look at another statement.

> THE LIE: "They *should* just get over it and grow up ...
>   but they *won't* ... idiots!"

> THE TRUTH: "I *wish* they would get over it ...
>   I *could* help, or I *could* just ignore them."

Yes, you *would like* it if they got over whatever the "it" is. That's your desire and opinion. You can have opinions and desires too, you know. They *could* get over it; they *could* just whine and complain. It's up to them. They choose. Choosing to do whatever it takes to "get over it" would be wiser, but they may, and can, choose to be foolish and play the victim. You, on the other hand, *could* offer to help, or you *could* decide the best thing is to keep your distance. There is no *one right way* this situation *should* be handled.

This example adds another dimension to relationships. If you tend to live by the *shoulds*, you are much more likely to try to make others live by the same list of *shoulds* and *shouldn'ts*. Misery loves company. If you have to be a serf toiling all day in the muck, no sense letting others go to the afternoon opera. You become very critical, demanding, demeaning, and condescending. You may not think you are. I wonder how those closest to you would answer?

It's not just a word game. When you exchange the *shoulds* for the *coulds*, you give yourself options.

> When you have options, real options, you have real choice.

> When you have choice, you have freedom.

> When you have freedom, you have the responsibility that comes with choosing.

> Sometimes that responsibility comes down to choosing between wisdom and foolishness.

> Most of the time though, it's a matter of choosing from several options that *all* have positive and negative elements to them. You are free to engage the brain

God gave you to choose freely.

If you choose foolishness over wisdom, you reap the consequences God and nature have already laid out. But you are *not* condemned as a person. If you choose wisdom, you can rejoice in the rewards. If you choose from among several viable options, you accept both the positive and negative aspects of that choice. Still no condemnation. If you make a mistake, you *could* learn from it. You *would like* to grow from that experience so that you do not have a repeat performance. You *could* …

You would probably agree with me that I *should* pay my taxes. That I *have* to. Who says I absolutely *have* to? Who says I absolutely *should*?

"The IRS says you *have* to."

Some Americans do *not* pay their taxes.

But they *have* to.

But, they *don't*. Some choose to try to get out of it. Some choose to work for cash only. The IRS can't get inside my body and make me pull out my checkbook. They can't *make* me pay.

They most certainly try to (and do) *influence* my thinking. They want me to *choose* to pay my taxes.

I *could* pay taxes. I *could* go to jail. I *could* run to Mexico.

> I will *choose* to pay
> my taxes.

> I *wish* there
> was another
> option!

I choose to pay my taxes, just like I choose to obey God – willingly. I want to obey Him. It's a *could*, not a *should*. It's a *want* to, not a *have* to. The outward action may end up being exactly the same, but the inward motivation is totally different. The *should* makes you a serf of the tyrant. The *could* makes you the son of the Father. And whether other people give you due credit or not, you still hold onto the truth that you *chose*. The *should* enslaves, the *could* frees. The *should* oppresses, the *could* empowers.

> "I guess we *should* get rid of all these here *shoulds* in our thinking, *shouldn't* we, Gerald?"

> "Think we really *should*?"

> "Yup, it's time we clean out our jukeboxes like the young man said."

> "Do I *have* to, Helen? I mean, do I really *have* to?"

> "Of course you *have* to. It's what you *should* do if you want to live in the present!"

Get a piece of paper

Cut it in half. On one piece, write *should* and *shouldn't*. On the other, write *could*, *would like to*, *I wish* and *I choose to*.

Lay both pieces out in front of you

Choose to keep one of the pieces of paper and destroy the other.

> "I know I *should* keep the 'could' piece, *shouldn't* I?"

> **THE FINE PRINT:** Realize whichever piece of paper you choose to destroy, you can *not* think or say those words anymore, ever!

> "But, Mr. Teacher Sir, *what if* I forget and say the words I *shouldn't*?"

See how sneaky the *what ifs* and the *shoulds* are? They can sneak in almost anywhere! You can choose the *could* words. If that is the paper you choose, destroy the *should* paper. Burn it, tear it up in little bits, eat it, whatever you want. Just destroy it. You can also choose to keep the *shoulds*, if you want. You choose.

Do the change out

Every time you have an opportunity to use *should* or *shouldn't*, stop yourself. Use one of the *could* phrases instead. It will take a conscious effort, but it will be worth it in the end. This change out will take anywhere from a few weeks to several months. Be patient and keep working. This is the nuts and bolts of how you go about transforming your mind.

Sandy was a seasoned expert at beating up on herself with *should* thinking. On one occasion, I played a "Let's Make a Deal" exercise with her. A couple days later she stopped mid-sentence and shot this I'd-like-to-kill-you look at me. She accused me of taking away half of her vocabulary! Without the use of the *shoulds*, she found herself speechless, which was a rare occasion for her. In the end she thanked me. She's still a friend. She even gave me permission to share her story!

Remember, freedom comes from knowing and *using* the truth. The *shoulds* are only perceptions, not the truth. C*ould*, while allowing you the freedom to choose error, equally gives you the opportunity to choose the truth. *Could* inspires, *should* erodes any confidence you have. *Should* strives for a perfect, idealistic, unattainable goal. *Could* strives for an excellent, realistic attainable reality. *Should* leaves no room for growth, it's all or nothing. *Could* pushes you onward, while still allowing room for growth and maturity. *Should* accepts no limitations whatsoever. *Could* recognizes legitimate limitations and accommodates expectations accordingly.

The *shoulds* need to die. The tyrant needs to be de-throned. The finger-in-your-face can be replaced with an arm around your shoulder. The choice is yours. You *could* live like a serf the rest of your life ("No! No!"). You could choose to walk away free ("Pick me! Pick me!"). The choice really is yours.

Beating the Anxiety Monster
CHAPTER 15

As I address the subject of anxiety, I realize that beginning with some basic definitions is critical. Over the years I have learned that words don't mean what they mean, and I'm continually going back to my dictionary to check out what the meaning of a word truly is. So I take you back to Uncle Webster for your vocabulary lesson of the day.

> "Can you tell us without using all those technical words, please, Mr. Teacher, Sir?"

ANXIETY 101, VOCABULARY LIST:

FEAR: An intense emotional reaction to a *legitimate* and *present* danger.

ANXIETY: An intense emotional reaction, usually of dread, to a *perceived/anticipated* and/or *future* danger.

PANIC: An ill-advised *behavioral reaction* when you have become overwhelmed by the emotion of fear or anxiety.

OBSESSIVE: A *persistent*, unwanted *thought* (or thought pattern) that is very difficult or impossible to stop.

OBSESSIVE COMPULSIVE: A disorder where you attempt to stop the obsessive thinking (see above) by engaging in a *repetitive behavior*, such as hand washing, counting, double-checking everything, cleaning, reciting words or phrases over and over again, etc.

WORRY: A non-technical term for anxiety.

CONCERN: The Christian-ized version of anxiety. The legitimate use of the term concern is often lost in this misuse. A horse by any other color is still a horse, whether or not you blessed the paint first.

Anxiety shows its colors in many different ways.

- Trembling or shaking
- Excessive worrying
- Feeling restless, keyed up or on edge
- Easily fatigued
- Hard to concentrate
- Problems sleeping
- Always having a "plan B," and "C" and …
- Avoiding situations or decisions that you are unsure about
- Feeling stuck and unable to make decisions without a lot of effort
- Afraid of being wrong
- Thinking, always thinking … planning … thinking …
- Having to know what is going to happen next
- Feeling of impending failure or rejection
- Being over controlling
- Feeling out of control
- Depressed

- Angry often, for no apparent reason

Anxiety is generated by a thinking pattern, a thinking *habit* – a very *bad* thinking habit to say the least. The phrase that echoes out of your jukebox is, *what if* …

> *What if* … I disappoint someone?

> *What if* … I make a mess of things?

> *What if* … I don't do everything the way I should?

> *What if* … I say something I *shouldn't*?

> *What if* … God really doesn't accept me? (I *should* be better.)

> *What if* …

The problem with *what if* thinking is your focus. Anxiety pulls your focus into the future and away from the present. Present tense fear says, "It *is* happening, *now!*" Anxiety, on the other hand says, "*What if* it happens (someday)?" Many of the things you have worried about over the years have never come to pass.

> "But, *what if* it does happen this time, Maynard?"

Anxiety focuses on the future, a future that does *not* exist yet, and may *never* exist the way you envision it in your mind. You cannot control the future. The more you focus on the future, the more out of control you will feel, *because it is out of your control*. The control that belongs to you is *only* in the present, because the present *does* exist. What you do today will have an influence on tomorrow, yes, but you cannot control any part of tomorrow yet. You cannot live tomorrow today. That comes tomorrow. You only have control of parts of today. Anxiety successfully rivets your thinking pattern on *perceived* and *future* possible dangers, and throws you out of control.

As I became aware of my own *what if* thinking (that ran through my mind from morning until night) I went about asking people for ways to stop the craziness inside my mind. All I got were the standard clichés:

"Just don't worry about tomorrow."

"Take every thought captive."

"Just think about the good things."

I was not sarcastic when I responded to each with an honest, "How?" They told me what I *should* be doing. I already knew that, but *how* could I get there? All I got were blank looks, but no answers. Nobody could tell me *how* to shut down the *what if* thinking pattern.

Breaking the *what if* thinking habit is much the same as breaking the *should* thinking habit.

(1)   Identify the *what if* that is ricocheting off the inner walls of your mind.

(2)   Stop the *what if* thought.

(3)   Replace it with the legitimate, present reality of *what is* …

To help me in this transition, I came up with a four-question technique. This technique is rather silly, but consider the source – a therapist! It works, though.

I put these four questions on a small card.

(1)   Name 5 colors I see right now.
(2)   Name 5 sounds I hear right now.
(3)   Name 5 things I physically feel right now. (i.e. watch on my wrist, wind in my hair, feet on the floor, etc.)
(4)   What do I need to do, or think about, RIGHT NOW?

I placed the card on my nightstand and answered the questions first thing in the morning, as soon as there were enough brain cells working.

I took the card with me to work and tried to review the four questions between three and five times, even if the day was going great. Habits are built on repetition, you know. Habits are built on repetition.

As I went to bed, I would place the card back on my nightstand and answer the questions one more time.

I had no idea whether this little technique, which I have nick-named "3 X 5 + 1" would do any good or not. I just knew I had to do something to try to slow down the *what if* thinking that was controlling me more than I was controlling it. What I did notice was that every time I went through this exercise, it helped, if only for a few minutes. I felt less anxious. Some days I was the victor, successfully stopping the onslaughts of the *what if;* other days the *what ifs* won. Over the period of time it takes to break a bad habit and establish another one in its place, the *what is* began to take root. In the course of about two to three months, the change out happened. Not only did the *what is* take root, it became the default thinking. It became more and more automatic.

"I'm healed, Sam! Lordy, does it feel good!"

The *what ifs* still sneak in sometimes, but not as often. And now that the *what is* is familiar to my thinking, the *what if* feels like a foreigner. I felt other changes too. The present became more alive to me, because I was *in* it rather than in the black hole of the future. I noticed more, felt lighter, remembered better. I also felt a whole lot more in control, because my focus was on present things I had control over, not future things I had no control over.

The first three questions use your physical senses to bring your focus out of the future and into the present. Colors, sounds and touching are in the present realm only. It's a way of getting your mind to consciously think about *what is* around you. The reason for five responses to these three questions is so I could keep track on my fingers! (Feel free to modify it in any way that will be more applicable to you.)

"*What if* that was only four colors? *What if* ..."

So often we think that whatever our thinking is thinking about is what we should think about.

"Say, what?"

"Sounds like that psycho-babble stuff that traveling minister warned us about last year, Lucy!"

Most people think that whatever is on their mind is the thought they need to dwell upon. If your mind were a Saint Bernard dog, it would be taking *you* for a walk right now, jerking you to this tree, "*what if*," then off to those bushes, "*what if*," etc., etc., etc. Your wandering thoughts are choosing what you think about. Wouldn't the walk be a whole lot better if *you* told the Saint Bernard where *you* were going to go and made the dog heel? When you answer the question "What do I need to do, or think about, RIGHT NOW?" *you* are choosing what you think about in the present. You decide which path to take. You are in control. If you want to study, then choose to study. If you need to take a shower, then shower, but don't shower *and* worry. If you are driving, then drive, and enjoy the drive. Count cars, look for out-of-state license plates, or just pay attention for once! Relax your brain. Think about only what is in front of you.

Depression

Anxiety is a serious issue because it's directly linked to depression. Think of the circuit breaker box in your house. If you were to plug all your appliances into one electrical socket and turn them on, you would blow a fuse and have a power outage. But if you did *not* have the breaker box and did the same foolish thing, you may likely have a fire on your hands. Thus, the reason for the circuit breaker box is to avoid destroying your house. Depression is much the same. Some depression has an organic basis to it. Psychologically induced depression has an anxiety basis to it. Anxiety and stress build until it's at a level that will bring emotional or physical destruction to your body. Your body makes an executive decision, without consulting you first, that says, "No way, Harry!" and shuts the power down. You have an emotional power outage called depression. To successfully treat clinical depression, you must also address underlying thinking patterns and conclusions that generate anxiety.

Anger

Anxiety is also at the root of anger. Anger is a secondary emotion, which means that it's made by combining two other emotions together. Good little Christians have been told that anger is wrong. So church-goers do a bit of verbal cosmetic surgery and say they are just "frustrated" or are simply "struggling." Again, a horse by any other color is still a horse. Check its teeth.

Behind anger, or frustration for those in divine denial, you will always find anxiety. The equation for anger looks like this:

$$HURT \ + \ ANXIETY \ = \ ANGER$$

Whenever you mix vinegar with baking soda you get the bubbles. Whenever you mix hurt/disappointment with anxiety (the *what ifs*) you get anger. The anger is noticeable and the hurt is fairly easy to discover, but the anxiety behind it all takes some searching to uncover. It may not even seem present at times, but it's there, nonetheless. Just as with depression, getting to the root cause of anger is critical. Anger management can help you learn to direct your anger toward an appropriate target. However, to actually decrease the cause of anger in the first place, you will once again need to take a closer look at the *what ifs* of your thinking.

Anxiety, depression and anger are all cousins with different last names, but they're all part of the same unhealthy mob family. Anxiety really is a monster. But look at it this way. You can kill three giants with the same stone and sling! The "3 X 5 + 1" technique will reduce the anxiety, one down. If you are less anxious overall, you are less likely to become overwhelmed and depressed, two down. With the anxiety reduced, you will become angry less often, three down.

"This is better than a free week at youth camp, Billy!"

This Thing Called "Forgiveness"

CHAPTER 16

WARNING: This chapter may be hazardous to your pre-conceived notions about the sweet little doctrine of forgiveness. Read this chapter at your own risk.

The Christians' answer to every human dilemma is the heal-it-all, fix-it-all, do-it-all spiritual thing called forgiveness. It was not until I took to a serious study of the subject, that I realized how little I knew, and was not taught, about the actual dynamic of forgiveness.

Forgiveness is *not* an event where you, the offended, utter pious words that somehow release the accused and yourself as well.

Forgiveness is *not* denying that the wrong ever occurred.

Forgiveness is *not* forgetting that the events of your past ever took place.

Forgiveness is *not* a spiritual way of saying that the wrong done to you is all right and of no consequence.

Forgiveness is *not* self-martyrdom. It's not a self-righteous attempt to look good while licking your wounds.

Forgiveness is *not* cheap, quick or easy.

Forgiveness is *not* automatically trusting or even liking the person who hurt you.

These are all the things that forgiveness is *not*. What *is* it then? Good question. At the risk of sounding like a sermon on paper, let me start by looking at the root meaning of the word in question, yes, in the Hebrew and Greek languages. I'm ignorant of the Bible languages; I just know how to cheat and use the back of my *Strong's Exhaustive Concordance*. (It looks good though!) What began to emerge from my study surprised me.

In the Hebrew, which is a picture language, the word forgiveness looks like this:

- To burn.
- To carry away.
- To bear or endure. (Interesting.)
- To pardon from penalty.
- To suffer. (Huh? I never knew this was a part of
        forgiveness!)
- To lift off the weight of burden.

Already there were some new twists to this idea of forgiveness that I had not heard before. As I moved on to the Greek, more began to unfold.

- To forsake.
- To lay aside.
- To put away. (Okay, I'm getting the picture here!)
- To yield up.
- To sustain damage. (Where did *this* one come from?)

- To send away from me.

As I tried to pull together a working definition from all these pieces, what resulted was something simple and clear:

> To *lift off* the weight of the debt, to *send it away*,
> and to absorb or *suffer the damage myself*.

I don't know if I like this definition all that well! I can accept the *lift off* and the *send it away* parts. The *suffer the damage myself* part is something I would prefer to ignore, thank you very much! That may be too hard to swallow. Can you remember a sermon (I'm sure you remember every sermon you ever heard!) that tied forgiveness and suffering into an understandable concept? If you can, count yourself blessed. I never have, even as an adult. I can remember statements to the effect of, "That's just your cross to bear." This is different.

Forgiveness is a process, not an event. It takes time for "process" to process. Healing and forgiveness both take time.

> The greater the wrong, the greater and deeper the pain.

> The deeper the pain, the greater the damage or injury.

> The greater the damage, the longer it takes to heal.

> The longer it takes to heal, the longer it takes to fully forgive.

No big physics formula here, just common sense.

The process of forgiveness follows six distinct stages. You may move through these stages in a linear fashion, one at a time.

Or you may bounce back and forth among them. Either way is fine.

The process will still include these stages:

(1)   Clearly state the actual wrong done to you.

(2)   With every wrong done, a debt is incurred.

(3)   Transfer the debt to God.

(4)   Your copy of the debt list gets marked "paid in full."

(5)   Absorb the damage.

(6)   Forgiveness is lived out in every day life.

Clearly state the actual wrong done to you

Yes, before you can even begin to forgive, you need to articulate the who, what, when and where that needs to be forgiven. Look at the story of Joseph in the book of Genesis. When he finally showed himself to his brothers, he articulated the wrong by saying, "I am your brother Joseph, the one you sold into Egypt!" There it is, the wrong stated plain and simple.

You may not *want* to identify the wrong clearly. It may bring back painful memories. It may feel like you are trying to blame somebody instead of being responsible for yourself. If you identify the actual wrong done against you, it may be bigger than you want to admit. On the other hand, it may *not* be as big as you have conjured it up to being in your eyes.

Differentiating between what is a specific, legitimate infraction of wrong and your opinion of a perceived wrong can be difficult. Was the wrong in question a breach of civil, biblical, or moral law? Being too busy as a father is not wrong. It's not wise, though. It yields negative results for the family, but it's not an infraction against any law. But failing to provide for the legitimate emotional needs of your children is morally and spiritually wrong. I'm not trying to play word games here. This is *not* just a matter of semantics; it's a matter of finding the truth. Finding the truth amidst all your emotions, opinions and perceptions can be hard to do. Nevertheless, it must be done if forgiveness is to be achieved. This is where an outside, objective perspective is invaluable.

> **CAR EXAMPLE:** I will try to use a simple example to walk you through each of the six stages. Between you and me, let's say you have become angry at me for something you read. In your anger you find my car and smash in the front windshield. (Please, this is just an illustration. Don't take this idea seriously!) When we go before the judge at the city courthouse, he will try to determine what was done wrong. The specific infraction you did against me is *breaking my windshield*. It's *not* getting angry at me; it's *not* disagreeing with me. The judge is not concerned about anger or disagreement, just the law that was broken. Statute 35, paragraph 21, sub-section 103 says, "Do not damage property that belongs to someone else." You broke my windshield. The wrong has been clearly stated.

With every wrong done, a debt is incurred

All of a sudden there is a you-owe-me that has come into existence. Manure draws flies. Wrongs draw debts. This may not sound very Christian, but it's true. When mankind, represented by Adam and Eve, sinned against God and ate of the forbidden fruit, a debt was incurred. A debt that was ultimately paid with the death of Jesus.

CAR: You were wrong to smash my windshield. Now, you owe me a new windshield. (Now, if I have a good lawyer, you will also owe me a million dollars for "pain and suffering"!) The wrong has been stated and the debt has been clarified.

Just as you need to clearly articulate the wrong done to you, you need to clearly define the debt that is owed you. Saying you owe me a new windshield is easy. Defining the debt within the context of a relationship is much harder.

The person who wronged you owes it to you to …

- Admit it actually happened, that he did it to you.

- Validate that it was wrong.

- Confess it was his fault. (Whether he intended to hurt you or not, it's still wrong. It's still his actions that caused the pain and therefore, his fault.)

- Repair whatever damage is repairable.

- Set the record straight with others who need to know.

- Ask for your forgiveness.

This notion that the person owes you may not set very well. But they *do* owe you. You *do* hold a you-owe-me list in your hand, even though you may not even know what is written on it. You need to know what is on the list in order for the forgiveness process to continue.

Forgiveness and confrontation are not mutually exclusive topics. If a wrong has been done, you are to confront the offending person. While you are confronting, you are also forgiving, because both begin with statements of the wrong done and the debt incurred. Confrontation shows them their offense, the debt they owe, and asks them to pay it back and absorb whatever damages can be absorbed. If they confess, repent and agree to cover the debt; it makes things much better and easier for you. You still have the pain to heal from. Trust still needs to be re-established. The process will still take time, but it will be a bit easier. If they refuse, you continue in the forgiving process for your own sake, as hard as it may be.

Sometimes a confrontation is *not* a good or wise course of action. If the person is still hurtful, manipulative or dangerous (physically, emotionally or spiritually), you may choose not to confront. Proverbs 9:7-8 says, "Whoever corrects a mocker invites insult; whoever rebukes a wicked man incurs abuse." Know anybody like this? "Do not rebuke a mocker or he will hate you;" is the logical and safe action. Or you may choose to use the legal system to do the confronting and to insure your safety. You may choose to forgo any form of confrontation and move on with the forgiving process. The choice is yours to make.

Transfer the debt to God

Now comes the hard part. You have a list of the wrongs done to you. You have a list of the you-owe-me's, and in doing so you have become the Debt-Collector. Wrongs need to be made right. God set the world up that way. His very character reflects that. Wrongs must be righted. The question is *who* will see to it that these specific wrongs, on this specific list, will be made right, and when? Who will be the Keeper of the Debts? It comes down to you or God.

Will you keep the debt list? Will you try to keep track of it until it gets paid? Do you want the job of Debt-Collector? Will you try to make them pay?

Or ...

Will you transfer the list to God? Will you let Him keep track of the wrongs and make sure they are made right? Will you leave it up to Him to see that the debts get marked paid in full? Will you let Him be the Debt-Collector?

For this to even be an honest choice, you have to believe that God will in fact right the wrongs, that He even cares, that He will not manage to lose the list under some heavenly cloud, or that He will flippantly say, "My grace is sufficient for you!" Is God even there, really? Does He care, really? Sunday school answers fall short here. What is the living truth? These are the heart questions that come to the surface when you are faced with a choice like this.

> **CAR:** You wronged me. You owe me. I choose to give the debt list to God. Count me out. I'm not here to collect on my windshield anymore. Now the issue is between you and God.

With forgiveness, you decide to transfer the debt into God's keeping, for Him to keep track of. Now the issue is between the other person and God. You are out of the loop altogether. You let go. You send it away from you, as a choice, as an agreement.

Your copy of the debt list gets marked "paid in full"

Once you give it away, they owe you nothing. They do *not* owe you one single thing, not an apology, not an "I'm sorry," *nothing*. Everything between you is covered with the "paid in full" that is in your own handwriting. This is why it's so hard to let go of the list. So many times we still want something from them, even a small something, anything to help us feel better, or vindicated. You may be too spiritual to seek vengeance, but you may harbor a secret desire to be there when God gives them their due! Check the motives of your heart.

> **CAR:** You wronged me. You owe me. I choose to give the debt list to God. Now the issue is between you and Him. When you walk out of the courthouse, you owe me absolutely nothing, not even a "good-bye." You are free of any and all obligation. You are free and clear in my eyes. I have marked my copy of the debt list "paid in full." The gavel has dropped, the judge is gone, and we go our separate ways.

> **SIDE NOTE:** If you decide however, to volunteer payment for my windshield, I will gladly accept your reimbursement! I will not reject your offer in order to look more spiritual! Let's get real here. I am allowed to accept your repentance and your money. And if you were to do so, it would make it easier for me to complete the forgiving process. But I'm not bound by your actions. I do not attempt to bind you to any specific action, either. I can forgive whether or not you cooperate.

This is the point where one of several myths about forgiveness spring to life. The myth is "If I really forgive the person, then I'm supposed to trust them. Right?" Wrong. Just because you have forgiven the offending person, does *not* mean you automatically trust them, like them or even want to be around them. I have forgiven you for smashing out my windshield, but I'm *not* going to park beside you in the church parking lot next Sunday! Why? Because forgiveness and trust are two different issues altogether.

Forgiveness begins with the letter "F," trust begins with "T." For all I know, you may still be angry and dangerous.

Back to the story of Joseph. The whole purpose of the money in the sacks of grain and needing to bring Benjamin to Egypt was a test. Joseph was checking to see if his brothers, who had been dangerous and untrustworthy the day they sold him into slavery, were able to be trusted today. Only after they proved themselves trustworthy, did he reveal himself to them. Forgiveness is yours to give. Trust is theirs to earn. Always.

Absorb the damage

If marking "paid in full" across the debt list is the hard part, absorbing the damage is the costly part.

> **CAR:** Once we leave the courthouse, you don't owe me anything. But what about my windshield? Has it magically been fixed by a couple of mechanically inclined angels? I don't think so. Who pays for a new windshield? *I* do. *I* pay the price. *I* absorb the damage. *I* suffer the inconvenience of all of this. *I* drive off to the repair shop with the wind in my face and the bugs in my teeth. No magic prayer here. With forgiveness, *I* spend the money and *I* do the work to get the windshield fixed.

To absorb the damage is *not* to say you absorb the *blame*. It is *not* your fault. **IT IS *NOT* YOUR FAULT.** It's *not* fair. Is this clear enough? It was *not* – it will never be – your fault. Period. Still, you chose to let go of the debt list anyway. Now, you have to do whatever it takes to bring healing and restoration to your broken heart and/or body. You take action rather than lying around like a wounded puppy waiting for them to bring the healing to you. Let me repeat. It's *not* your fault, it's *not* fair and you are *not* accepting the blame for the infraction. You are simply absorbing the cost of healing and becoming whole again.

Two things make absorbing the damage even harder: (1) When the offense is still going on today. In this case, you may need to get as far away from the person as you can. (2) When some of the damage is permanent and irreversible, either physically or relationally. Some injuries heal but still leave you scarred for life. When this happens, you need to reach deeper into your soul to be able to extend the forgiveness that will set you free.

Forgiveness is lived out in everyday life

After you have given up keeping track of the debt list, you *act* as though they do not owe you from that point on. While you may not trust them, you do not remind them of the infraction, verbally or non-verbally, overtly or covertly, seriously or sarcastically. Whenever you see them you act out the reality that the copy of your debt list has been marked "paid in full." You treat them with the respect you would extend to any human being even though the pain may still be present in your heart. This is what true forgiveness is. True forgiveness brings true freedom. It may take you days, weeks or even years to get from beginning to end. So be it. Be careful not to compare another person's progress to your own. Each case is different and unique. While the progression is similar, the pace is not.

Enter another myth we often teach about forgiveness. "If I truly forgive the other person then the relationship is supposed to be reconciled and everything be fine. Right?" Wrong again.

Reconciliation is derived from the same root word as the word "confess," which means, "to say the same thing." The only way you will have a reconciled bank account is if you say "I have $50,000 in my account" and the bank says "You have $50,000 in your account." The parties involved – you and the bank – both *say the same thing*. But if you say "I have $5,000 in my account" but the bank says "You have $500 in your account." Guess what? Your account is *not* reconciled. And it will *never* be reconciled until … both sides *say the same thing*. One party cannot create reconciliation. It's a two-way street.

> **CAR – one last time:** I have genuinely forgiven you, and released you from owing me anything. But you aren't willing to admit that you ever broke out my windshield. You will never admit that my broken windshield is/was your debt to pay. Guess what? We're *not* reconciled.
>
> So, not only do I not trust you, but also the relationship is broken and/or strained because of the lack of reconciliation on your part.

Time will never give birth to reconciliation. Likewise, forgiveness alone can never birth reconciliation. Reconciliation is when the offending party clearly and honestly states the wrong done and debt that's been acquired as well. You both *say the same thing*. That's why stages 1 and 2 are so critical, so you know what the "same thing" is that needs to be said by both sides. Then, and only then, can the reconciliation process begin. Forgiveness starts with "F" and … you got it … reconciliation begins with "R." They are *not* the same.

You can forgive without there being reconciliation just like you can forgive without automatically trusting the other person. But you can't have reconciliation without forgiveness and trust being reestablished first – at least not real reconciliation.

Finding God in the Rubble
CHAPTER 17

This has been the hardest chapter of all for me to write. Not because I don't know where God is, but the journey into His presence can't be reduced to words very easily. And besides, you have heard all the words, acrostics and examples already. Expressing this concept without it sounding like another "thou shalt" is no easy task.

Finding God without getting lost in the maze of the religious jargon can be tricky. Being drawn into God's presence without being pulled into organizational politics is not easy. But if there really is a God (and I firmly believe there is), I want to find Him and know Him better. I know all *about* Him. I know what others say *about* Him. I know what I think *about* Him. But I want to know *Him*, the being that lives and talks and moves.

Rather than tell you what to do or how to do it (I'm sure you have a shelf full of books that are more than willing to do this already) let me simply tell a bit of my story … my journey … from one lab rat to another.

Almost 16 years ago, I happened across a little book – the only one left on the shelf – entitled *Experiencing the Depths of Jesus Christ*. I picked it up. The author was a 17th Century French woman named Jeanne Guyon. This was my introduction into the arena of silence, contemplation and surrender. I will not attempt to match Guyon's eloquence on the subject of experiencing the presence of The Almighty. Here, though, are some thoughts I have catalogued along my journey out of the rubble:

God is not who I thought He was

I had heard about God all my life. I knew both sides of every doctrinal argument. I knew what my parents thought. I knew what others thought. I knew what I thought I thought. But I was not ready for a God who was so alive and real that He refused to be contained in my systematic theology box.

As long as God remained a doctrine to be studied, organized and defended, I was bigger. I was safe. I could take Him or leave Him. But when He became the God of the universe standing in front of me, I could do nothing to contain Him. He was bigger and I was afraid. Words fall short in my attempt to express this thought, but in short, God did not fit into any of the boxes I had made for Him. He was not who I thought He was.

God does love me

This point may sound too obvious to even mention, but it's where God began with me. I know, and have known, all the songs and verses that tell me God loves me. But does He *really*? Does He really love *me*? Does He love me *all* the time? How *could* He love me with all my hang-ups, times of being angry at Him, times I ditched Wednesday night prayer meeting and all the other things He and I know about?

Then come the questions like, would He really *want* to love me

… I mean, really? Not because He's "God" and is supposed to love me, but simply because He wants to.

If you want something crazy, this is it. A sovereign King making a unilateral decision, solely for my benefit, that is limitless and cannot be broken or messed up by anyone (including me). He paid for it, it has no end, and it will not be recalled. This is a crazy kind of love, and it is all true! This is how *He* defines His love for me.

As God whispered, "Yes. Yes. Yes." to all of these questions, my "Yeah, buts … " started shouting back at Him.

- "Yeah, but I'm a nobody."
- "Yeah, but I'm not perfect. Look at all this junk …"
- "Yeah, but I'm not really good at anything."
- "Yeah, but You need to focus on other people, not me."

One day, I took I Corinthians 13:4-8 and wrote it out as a letter to me from God. I have since misplaced it, but it began something like this:

"Dear Tim,
        I am patient with you. I care about you. I'm not arrogant, I won't act c o n d e s c e n d i n g l y toward you. I won't be rude to you …
Love God."

Slowly, I began to trust His words (at least a little). You can too. I wish I could victoriously say that I've slain the demon of "yeah but" … but the truth it that those thoughts occasionally find their way back into my mind. It's a whole lot less often than it used to be. And God still whispers "Yes. Yes. Yes."

God is personal, not institutional

Next came the verses from Romans 8:38-39, which I rewrote in a similar way:

> "Tim,
>> Nothing, *nothing*, not the wrongs you have done, not your stubbornness, nor your impatience, not what has happened to you, not circumstances, not refusing to go into the ministry, no 'yeah, buts …,' not the challenging you do … nothing can separate you from My love. Nothing can make Me stop loving you. *Nothing*.
>
> God."

This is *not* a do-this-and-I-will-accept-you kind of arrangement. It's an I-love-you-because-I-want-to-period crazy kind of friendship that makes no human sense. It does make sense to God though, because this *is* how much He cares for us. I have yet to get to the bottom of His love for me. I'm beginning to believe that maybe there honestly is no bottom, no end, no limit, no termination of His love for me.

Writing out these verses was a great beginning, but what came next I don't think I can adequately explain. I can't remember the exact time or circumstances that led, pushed or pulled me into the biggest risk I've ever taken. For some reason on that particular evening, I whispered "God, hold me." It wasn't a theological prayer … it was a cry of desperation. It wasn't preplanned or practiced … it was out of impulse that came from my soul. My mind and body became still and quiet long enough for God to approach. I pulled an old quilt around me and let myself be held – just like I'd held my girls when they were little and scared or hurt.

Guyon's words on becoming still began taking root and God *did* come close and His arms *did* hold me.

> One of the reasons I get so angry at cliches is that they take a good concept and make it cheap. When I talk about God "holding me" there's all kind of "junk" that can get in the way of what I'm really trying to say. I'm not talking about theology or metaphors or sentimental word pictures ... I'm trying to convey a real and personal awareness of the senses – as aware as you are of holding this book. Ugggg! There's no good words. Please try to read past the words as best you can. But this is how real ... how spiritually tangible ... God is and wants to be.

Let me keep going. Maybe it will make more sense as you read on.

God entered into my world

As His personal love began to take hold of my heart, it took me a while to realize that He had entered into *my* world, where I was. He was seeing *my* world, feeling *my* feelings and touching *my* pain. He, of all people, came into the lab rat cage and sat with *me*. I didn't have to be on my knees with my hands folded. I didn't have to close my eyes. It didn't have to be on Sunday only. I wasn't restricted to meeting Him at the altar or during my official devotions.

When He entered in, He did not condemn! He did not take the role of a boot camp drill instructor with a stern face, conducting some kind of spiritual white-glove inspection. He did not force Himself on me. Likewise, He will not minimize your pain, fear, confusion, questions or dreams.

As I was working on this particular part of this chapter, David Gatewood relayed a personal experience to me illustrating the *opposite* of how God operates. He had been in the field of Christian counseling for about ten years and had finally gotten his pastor-father to attend a Christian Association for Psychological Studies convention. He was thrilled. Finally, he could show his dad *his* world and what *he* did for a living and a ministry. Fifteen minutes into the opening presentation, his father looked at his watch, turned to David and said, "I think I have some other business I need to attend to. There's some fundraising I probably should do." As he excused himself from the convention, he punctuated his good-bye with, "You don't mind, *do you*?" His own father could not, or would not, tolerate his son's world. David remembered how it crushed him, how it devastated him to the point that it brought tears to his eyes.

Not so with God. Again, an old verse came alive to me, "I will never leave you; never will I forsake you." (Heb. 13:5). *Never.* I have walked alone all my life, but now I can let Him walk with me. He wants to. My view of God has changed from the football field where the coach stands on the sidelines pushing, yelling and driving me, to a mountain peak where the climbing guide encourages, respects and helps me up. We climb together. God has been willing to enter my world all along. I was the one who kept Him out … because I was afraid.

Was letting God that close risky? Yes! Was I scared out of my wits? Most of the time. Was it worth it? Yes! Keep reading.

God pulls me into His world

Slowly, I began to believe He *did* want the best for me. Gradually, I began to trust Him. I stopped going to other sources to find out about Him and began going directly to Him. I began to sit quietly, training my mind to be still. Sometime later, the prayer of "God,

I want to see You like *You* see You" was added to my "God, hold me" prayer. He was pulling me into His world.

> **ANOTHER DISCLAIMER:** I am *not* a believe-whatever-you-want-to-believe person. Nor am I an experience-validates-Scripture person. What I am attempting to say is that you need to look past the *form* to the real *function* of things. You need to focus not on the *place*, but the *person* of God Himself. You need to journey past the *ecclesiastical* and onto the *experiential*.

Each time He pulled me deeper into Himself, it revealed more and more of my own fears.

- Fears about being wrong
- Fears about being too "liberal"
- Fears about not having enough faith
- Fears about not being good enough

At this point, a third prayer was added: "God, let me see *me*, like *You* see me." The first prayer scared me big time, (the second one seemed safe) but this one terrified every fiber of my being.

- *What if* I'm not good enough?
- *What if* He rejects me?
- *What if* ...

Silence was hard for me. Not just having the environment quiet, but the quieting of my thoughts and mind. I was not used to His world. I did not know the "rules."

- *What if* He doesn't answer?
- *What if* I don't have enough faith?
- *What if* I'm wrong?

Silence, I have learned, is the outward expression of surrender. Maybe this is why we avoid silence so much. We often talk about the idea of surrender, how we *should* surrender, but actual surrender is different. Silence means:

- I have *no* choice, *no* voice, *no* say so.
- I have *no* defense for myself. I'm totally vulnerable!
- It's *His* world, not mine, and I need to listen to Him.
- *He* sets the agenda, not me.
- I have no control over this world, but *He* does.
- God speaks, I listen.

But in the silence of His world, He speaks life to my soul.

- He does *not* condemn me, even though I often do.
- He does *not* get impatient with me.
- He does *not* reject me.
- He does *not* hate me.
- He does *not* expect me to be perfect, even though I do.
- He does *not* expect me to pretend.
- He *wants* me to be, and feel, safe.
- He *does* love me.
- I *am* acceptable to Him now, just as I am.
- I have *not* disappointed Him.
- He *is* angry about all the wrongs inflicted upon me.
- He *does* see all the hypocrisy, and He hates it too.

He'll speak the same to you.

When I ran away from His world and back into mine, He stayed with me. We would walk in my world and, on occasion, He would pull me back into His. Now, whatever world I find myself in, I know I'm not alone. He is my God and nothing can take me away from Him.

Is it still risky? Yes, but it's easier to take the risk. Do I still get scared? Yes, but less often (that's a big relief). Is it still worth it? Yes. It really, really is. Keep reading …

God is mine

As I have experienced genuine growth, God has become personal to me. I know Him directly, not second hand. He is not a friend of a friend of mine, He is *my* friend. I also know Him as the Almighty, and I tremble with a healthy respect for Him. He has become *my* God. Nobody can take Him from me now. The church cannot, the denomination cannot, the world cannot, friends cannot, my parents cannot, my family cannot and hell itself cannot (even though it has tried, literally). He is mine. I know Him. I love Him. He loves me. You can take my reputation away from me, you can take my job or my finances or my family or my health, even my life, but you *cannot* take my God away from me. This is not theology … it is life and death for me. It's not the "right" answer because that's what Christian books are made of … it's the only answer. He's mine! I'm not alone anymore. It's become real for me.

I found God, not in the pew, but on my office sofa, late at night, with the lights out and a quilt over my legs. I found Him, not by study, but by sitting and letting the verses I learned as a child speak to me. I found Him, not by listening to a great preacher, but by being silent long enough to hear God's still small voice push past my own thoughts. Actually, He found me. I simply stopped running.

One last disclaimer. I am *not* against church, preaching, Sunday school or Bible study. All of these things are part of my life and I enjoy them, most of the time. But maybe, like me, you have trouble finding God in these places. Maybe like me, you need to find him on a sofa, or in a meadow, or listening to worship songs, or in the pages of your journal. I needed to go outside the *shoulds*. Maybe you do too.

Wherever you need to look, look. Sometimes we can't see the forest for the trees. Sometimes we, who grew up inside the sanctuary, need to go outside the hallowed halls to finally see the truth. That's just how it is for some of us. Maybe for you too.

It's *never* too late to sift through the rubble. It's *never* too late to look honestly into the jukebox of your mind. It's *never* too late to chase the holy heresies out of your parsonage thinking. It's *never* too late to heal the hurts. In my years in ministry and as a therapist, there's not much I haven't seen or heard. I know, it's *never* too late. *NEVER.*

I still pray "God, hold me" … and He still does.

The tyrant needs to be de-throned. The finger-in-your-face can be replaced with an arm around your shoulder. The choice is yours. You *could* live like a serf for the rest of your life ("No! No!"). You *could* choose to walk away free ("Pick me! Pick me!"). The choice really is yours.

APPENDIX
IDEAS FOR KEEPING A JOURNAL

1.   There are *no* rules. There is no "This is the way you *should* do it!"

2.   You do not have to make an entry every day, or keep a record of the entire day's events. This journal is for *your* benefit; there is no need to become enslaved by it. Feel the freedom to let days – even weeks or months – go by between entries. Write as the need or desire arises.

3.   Write what you are actually thinking. Put it into words as best you can. Write your feelings, thoughts, questions and opinions – the "inside" stuff. Nothing is unacceptable to put down. If you are thinking or feeling it, write it. You are being honest and open with yourself.

4.   Don't "edit" what you write. You don't need to write using complete sentences. There's no need to worry about spelling. Your entry doesn't even have to make sense. It can be pictures, diagrams, scribbles, whatever is needed at the moment ... for you.

5.   If you are concerned about someone reading your journal with its feelings and thoughts about other people, use

the first initials of their names or some other symbol you understand.

6. Keep your journal in a safe place. If you are writing what is in your mind and in your heart, guard yourself, by guarding your journal. Share your journal only when you want to, with whom you want, and for the purposes you want.

7. If it doesn't work for you, quit.

THE HOLY HERESIES THAT PK/MKs OFTEN DEVELOP

Make your marks using this scale:

1 = Not true at all
2 = Somewhat true
3 = Mostly true
4 = Almost always true

1 2 3 4   1) **"I HAVE TO BE PERFECT."** I feel (or was told) that "image is everything."

1 2 3 4   2) **"I SHOULD ALREADY KNOW."** I feel I was born mature and that I *should* already know.

1 2 3 4   3) **"I'M HERE FOR OTHERS."** It seems my job is to make other people comfortable.

1 2 3 4   4) **"I'M DIFFERENT."** I seem to live with a different set of expectations and rules than others.

1 2 3 4   5) **"I CAN'T TRUST ANYONE."** I *know* what people and churches are *really* like under the surface and I don't trust them.

1 2 3 4   6) **"I CAN RUIN MY DAD'S MINISTRY."** I have been told this or felt it often.

1 2 3 4   7) **"OTHER PEOPLE'S NEEDS ARE MORE IMPORTANT THAN MY OWN."** I feel that my needs are less important than others' needs.

1 2 3 4   8) **"I'M DAMNED IF I DO AND DAMNED IF I DON'T."** I feel that I have to go along with everything or I am against everything.

1 2 3 4   9) **"GOD IS DISAPPOINTED WITH ME."** I'm not perfect and I feel I should be. Sometimes I feel as if He hates me because I'm "bad."

IMPACTING FORCES ON PK/MKs

As a PK/MK, you had many impacting forces on your life. Please take a few minutes to review those impacting forces (to this date) as they fit into the four categories listed on the left-hand side. Assign a percentage to each. The four numbers should total 100% at the bottom.

Take the percentages from the left and divide the total into what you would describe as "good" or "bad" for each category.

[   ] **FAMILY**   [   ] The good [   ] The bad

[   ] **CHRISTIAN**   [   ] The good [   ] The bad
    COMMUNITY

[   ] **CULTURE (S)**   [   ] The good [   ] The bad

[   ] **OTHER STUFF** [   ] The good [   ] The bad

_____
100%

THE DEMOGRAPHIC STUFF

Check one: ___PK   ___MK ___Parachurch-Kid

Age: _____   Age when your parents began ministry _____

Number of years as a PK/MK _____   Male/Female (Circle one.)

Age when you **left home** or your parents ended ministry _____

Number of siblings _____   Your place in the birth order _____

Are you in ministry now? ___ Yes ___ No

Mail your responses on the Holy Heresies and Impacting Forces/Demographic Stuff to:

Timothy L. Sanford, M.A., c/o LifEdvice
info@lifedvice.com

READING LIST

Experiencing the Depths of Jesus Christ, Jeanne Guyon, The SeedSowers, 1975

False Assumptions, Dr. Henry Cloud and Dr. John Townsend, Zondervan Publishing House, 1994

False Intimacy, Dr. Harry W. Schaumburg, NavPress, 1992

Growing Up Holy and Wholly, Donald E. Sloat, Wolgemuth & Hyatt, Publisher, Inc., 1990

Letters Never Sent, Ruth Van Reken, "Letters", 1988

Life Together, Dietrich Bonhoeffer, Harper & Row, 1954

Notes on How to Live in the World ... And Still Be Happy, Hugh Prather, Doubleday, 1986

Powerful Personalities, Tim Kimmel, Focus on the Family, 1993

Ragamuffin Gospel, Brennan Manning, Multnomah Books, 1990

Safe People, Dr. Henry Cloud and Dr. John Townsend, Zondervan Publishing House, 1995

Safe Places, Stephen Arterburn, Frank Minirth and Paul Meier, Thomas Nelson, Inc., 1997

Search for Significance, Robert McGee, Rapha Publishing, Second Printing 1990

Second Row Piano Side, Chonda Pierce, Beacon Hill Press of Kansas City, 1996

Telling Yourself the Truth, William Backus and Marie Chapian, Bethany Fellowship, Inc., 1980

The Sacred Romance, Brent Curtis and John Eldredge, Thomas Nelson, Inc., 1997

Wild at Heart: Discovering a Life of Passion, Freedom and Adventure, John Eldredge, Thomas Nelson, Inc., 2001

The Wounded Healer, Henri J.M. Nouwen, Image Books, 1972

Toxic Faith, Stephen Arterburn and Jack Felton, Oliver-Nelson, 1991

When I Relax I Feel Guilty, Tim Hansel, David C. Cook Publishing Co., 1981

Why Christian Kids Leave the Faith, Tom Bisset, Thomas Nelson Publishers, 1992

Abba's Child, Brennan Manning, Navpress, 1994

A Violent Grace, Michael Card, Multnomah Publishing, 2000

The Spiritual Guide, Michael Molenous, The SeedSowers, 1982

You Know You're an MK When ..., Andy & Deborah Kerr, 1997

"I HAVE TO BE PERFECT"
(And Other Parsonage Heresies)

Was your father or mother a pastor, evangelist, rabbi, denominational superintendent, worship minister, missionary or key leader of a para-church organization?

If so, then this book is for you ... not *about* you, *for* you.

Whether you think your experience was good or bad, the truth is, it was both.

Tim Sanford is a missionary's kid, an ordained minister and an author who is in private practice as a licensed professional counselor. He has seen it all, heard it all, and now touches it all with candor, honesty, sarcasm and power. Tim opens up the mind of the PK, and helps you take an honest, deep look at the conclusions you may have drawn from your own PK experiences.

Questions or feedback: info@lifedvice.com

Made in the USA
San Bernardino, CA
17 June 2016